COME AND SEE
Resources For Lent

By **RANDOLPH W. BARR**
And **ANNE-ROSE REEVES**

C.S.S Publishing Co., Inc.
Lima, Ohio

COME AND SEE

Copyright © 1992 by
The C.S.S. Publishing Company, Inc.
Lima, Ohio

All rights reserved. No part of this publication may be reproduced, stored in a retrieval system, or transmitted in any form or by any means, electronic, mechanical, photocopying, recording, or otherwise, without the prior permission of the publisher. Inquiries should be addressed to: The C.S.S. Publishing Company, Inc., 628 South Main Street, Lima, Ohio 45804.

Library of Congress Cataloging-in-Publication Data

Barr, Randolph W., 1948-
   Come and see : resources for Lent / by Randolph W. Barr and Anne-Rose Reeves.
     p.   cm.
   ISBN 1-55673-385-2
   1. Lent. 2. Lent—Drama. 3. Lenten sermons. 4. Sermons, American. 5. Bible—Criticism, interpretation, etc. I. Reeves, Anne Rose, 1954-   . II. Title.
BV85.B33 1992   91-35308
263'.92—dc20   CIP

9203 / ISBN 1-55673-385-2   PRINTED IN U.S.A.

To all who helped us make this project a reality — Sandy Barr, Earle Reeves, Art and Lois Tress, The Rev. Dr. Richard Thulin, The Rev. Dr. Stephen Folkemer, The Rev. Dr. Mark Oldenburg, and the people and staff of St. Timothy Lutheran Church.

Prologue

There is a story in the Gospel of John in which the disciple Philip invites a man named Nathanael to follow Jesus, but Nathanael reacts to the invitation with disparaging doubt: "Can anything good come out of Nazareth?" This Lenten resource emerges from our own struggle to answer Nathanael's question.

Come And See is an invitation to the Christian community to celebrate and explore their gifts, vocations and sense of call. It is a practical means for Lenten discipleship that focuses not so much on individual acts of piety and repentance but on discipleship lived out within a communal context. Using texts from Mark and the lectionary year "C" as the biblical foundation for our resource, we offer a number of strategies for congregational leaders. The strategies enable people to "come and see" what they do in the name of Jesus. They include a pre-Lenten Mission Fair, which offers concrete means for Lenten discipleship, mid-week Lenten programs of worship and study, and sermons for Ash Wednesday and the Sundays in Lent. The strategy descriptions are rooted in actual practice and reflect our experiences in congregational settings. They may be used in their entirety or as modular pieces. Each can stand alone as a useful tool for parish ministry. Used in their entirety, however, the strategies provide a holistic approach to help Nathanael and us explore our doubts about the call to follow Jesus on the path of the kingdom.

Table Of Contents

Introduction

Introduction   11

The Mission Fair   16

Section 1 — Playlets

Introduction   21

1 — Lord, Everyone Is Searching For You   23
Evangelism Playlet

2 — What Are They Doing To My Sabbath?   33
Worship Playlet

3 — Can You See The Harvest?   40
Educational Ministries Playlet

4 — And They Cast Out Many Demons   48
Social Concerns Playlet

5 — The Lord Of The Storm   55
Stewardship Playlet

Section 2 — Bible Study

Introduction   65

1 — Evangelism Bible Study   66

2 — Worship Bible Study   68

3 — Education Bible Study   70

4 — Social Concerns Bible Study   72

5 — Stewardship Bible Study   74

Section 3 — Sermons

    Introduction   79

    Ash Wednesday Sermon   80
    Come And See . . . The Day Of The Lord

    First Sunday In Lent Sermon   84
    Come And See . . . The Wilderness

    Second Sunday In Lent Sermon   89
    Come And See . . . The King Who Weeps

    Third Sunday In Lent Sermon   93
    Come And See . . . The Way Of God

    Fourth Sunday In Lent Sermon   98
    Come And See . . . What The World Is Coming To

    Fifth Sunday In Lent Sermon   104
    Come And See . . . The Difference Of God

Some Last Things

    Epilogue   109

Introduction

Introduction
The Mission Fair

Introduction

How do the men and women of God decide whether they should join the evangelism committee or become assistant ministers for Sunday worship? How can they explore whether they have the gift to minister to the sick and dying without committing themselves for the whole year? How do Christian people find out whether they have the gift to teach Sunday school? At times, these questions are answered out of an individual's past experience and interest in one or another of the church's ministries. At other times, the invitation to explore new ways of discipleship comes from the pastor or a friend who is involved in a particular task of the church's life. While all these ways play an important role in the life of the congregation, we have asked ourselves whether we might be able to create a context in which our people can explore their gifts, vocations, avocations, and sense of call through a holistic approach. We believe that we have created such an approach in this resource. We have combined a variety of teaching, worship and program strategies to be used during the Epiphany and Lenten seasons. Our theme is to invite men and women to "Come and See" the diverse experiences and gifts of the people of God. We provide opportunities for sharing in these experiences on a trial basis. We celebrate. We struggle with the question of how the call to discipleship can be lived out amidst cultural expectations on our time and resources. And most important, we focus attention on God's graciousness as he enables all of us to minister to one another in Jesus' name.

The manner in which this resource attempts to encompass these goals is outlined as follows.

A. "Come And See" is a way of celebrating discipleship.

The celebration begins with a Mission Fair on the second Sunday after Epiphany. It is a show-and-tell event where those involved in congregational and community ministries are invited to set up displays and provide information and materials about the work they do. While the primary focus of the Mission Fair is to invite others to explore the possibility of participating in one or another ministry, the event also serves as a celebration and affirmation of the richness and diversity of the gifts of God to his people. Often such public celebration of discipleship is restricted to the worship or fellowship life of the congregation. The installation of committee chairpersons and Sunday school teachers is an annual event in many churches. Other congregations affirm regular leadership through annual dinners where awards for faithful service are presented. We believe that the Mission Fair goes a step further. It provides the arena in which respect, support and encouragement for the people's ministries are given and allows the people of God to tell their stories of how God empowers them for mission.

Storytelling from ministry is also the theme of our midweek Lenten dramas. The resource contains five playlets. Each one highlights a different ministry or program of the church. The worshiping congregation watches a group of their own members talk about and struggle with the expression of their gifts and talents. Outsiders in search of Jesus intrude upon these struggling disciples. Thus, the celebration of the gifts of the people that begins with the Mission Fair and moves through Lent, affirms successes, frustrations, struggles and doubts of the faithful.

B. "Come And See" is a means to provide ownership for the ministries of the people.

The primary focus here is not so much in upholding how individuals contribute to the welfare of the congregation itself but rather how the congregation as a whole serves the wider community in Christ's name. As Christ's disciples we are called to go out into the world to proclaim the good news and to minister to the neighbor. Many of our people do this by volunteering at social service organizations or by being involved in projects that seek justice and peace for God's people. The church does not always provide support of such expressions of discipleship. Again, the Mission Fair serves as the context for this focus. Displays and information about various community organizations to which individual members contribute their time and talent are interspersed with ministries of the congregation. In this manner, the Mission Fair concretely demonstrates the church's call to minister to the world. It also calls the congregation to remember the centrality of God's graciousness that enables his people to be faithful to this call.

C. *"Come And See" is a way to teach about the ministries of God's people.*

In the previous sections of this introduction we have already discussed how both the Mission Fair and the Lenten dramas serve to tell the stories of the joys and struggles that our call to discipleship entails. These stories not only celebrate, they also teach. The displays and materials of the Mission Fair teach about the goals, methods and needs of the various ministries. The Lenten dramas teach about the personal struggles of those involved in the various ministries. In order to address this particular aspect of the work of the ministries of the congregation more fully, we have also developed a five-week Bible study. Using Markan texts we ask our people to speak about their own struggles as they strive to deepen their sense of discipleship. Our questions aim at exploring the tension between necessities of daily life and Jesus' demands for discipleship. The Gospel of Mark is especially suited for this endeavor since one of its primary themes centers on the struggle of Jesus' disciples to understand their Lord and to follow in his footsteps. The Bible study may be used in conjunction with the Lenten dramas where modern-day disciples struggle with issues of incomprehension, temptations and a faith in Jesus who defies all expectations. Overall, then, the teaching aspect of this resource has a two-fold aim: First, it provides a realistic picture of the ministries of the people; and second, it invites everyone to explore their own potential call to reflect on or participate in such work.

D. *"Come And See"* gives ways and means for Lenten discipleship.

The primary goal of the resource is to provide a context in which individuals can explore their gifts and sense of call. We have already looked at the task of reflection through mid-week Lenten dramas and Bible study. We have spoken to the need for celebration and affirmation in the Mission Fair. The focus of this section then, is to look at practical and concrete ways in which discipleship may be explored. To do so we have chosen the Mission Fair and the season of Lent as our foundation. The Lenten season calls the people of God to remember the covenant of baptism and to immerse themselves in a series of disciplines for the sake of strengthening and renewing the faith. The Mission Fair serves as the vehicle for this task. Each person, upon entering the fair, receives a Lenten calendar in which he or she may mark a variety of commitments which the various ministries have prepared for the fair:

- Bring a bag of groceries for the local food pantry.
- Deliver altar flowers to a shut-in.
- Attend a specific ministry committee meeting for one evening to explore the possibility of whether this ministry may be suited for one's gift.

The goal of such disciplines is to enable people to explore their individual gifts on a trial basis while at the same time maintaining the focus on the community as a whole. Further, this approach allows the people of God to explore their discipleship at their own pace and level of comfort. Some people may wish to make many commitments whereas others may choose only a few. In choosing the Lenten season rather than the busy fall start-up, we lessen the pressure that often accompanies the demand for long-term commitments during the fall and winter stewardship campaigns. Nevertheless, the chance to explore a variety of ministries during Lent can serve as a foundation for conversation as the church prepares for a full stewardship emphasis.

E. *"Come And See" is a holistic approach.*

For parish leaders the *Come And See* resource may serve as a planning guide for both the Epiphany and Lenten seasons. As mentioned above, our approach encompasses teaching and worship forms as well as a Mission Fair. All focus upon exploring and deepening discipleship. Depending upon the size and activity of the congregation, parish leaders may wish to use the resource in its entirety or only use those elements which are suitable to the individual congregation.

We have included additional program ideas to enhance the fullness of *Come And See*. For example, a service of Affirmation of Baptism could be scheduled on the Sunday prior to the Mission Fair, Baptism of Our Lord. Mid-week worship and study can be strengthened with a simple meal. A post-Easter celebration of Lenten discipleship can be scheduled. Several other practical suggestions are included in the resource.

Finally, for parish pastors, we have prepared a series of sermons for Ash Wednesday and the Sundays in Lent. Texts are used in a manner consistent with the overall resource theme. Here the focus is on a progression from where we are to where we are going. It is the same theme that appears in the gospel for the Mission Fair Sunday: A man named Nathanael is invited by the disciple Philip to follow Jesus, but Nathanael has his doubts. "Can anything good come out of Nazareth?" he asks. "Come and see!" Thus Nathanael is asked to walk with Jesus on the path of the kingdom. We invite parish leaders and all of the men and women of God to do the same.

The Mission Fair

A. Overview.
On the Second Sunday after Epiphany, members and visitors arrive to find the church transformed into an exhibit hall. Lots of activity surrounds the balloons, display booths and the excitement of the people. A path is marked throughout the building with footsteps going from booth to booth.

Greeters and a large poster at the front door announce that today is the Mission Fair. Questions and all kinds of conversation fill the air. Each fair-goer is given a name tag, a Lenten calendar, and other equipment for use during the morning. Wandering from booth to booth, the fair-goer can hear stories about the exciting but often hidden ministries of the people of God. One church member has set up her booth because she volunteers at the hospital. The next table has Boy Scouts in their uniforms talking with folks about recycling aluminum cans. Further down the hall there are some women inviting people to deliver altar flowers to shut-ins. Even the parish nurse is there trying to find people to help in her programs of care throughout the community.

The footprints through the building lead to new information about the multitude of ministries going on in the congregation and in the parish. But there is more. All the fair-goers are challenged to explore new gifts for ministry within themselves. There is also the possibility to use existing gifts in new ways.

One fair-goer leaves with a notation on her calendar that she will deliver flowers to shut-ins on the Third Sunday in Lent. A young confirmand goes home with information about recycling aluminum cans and a commitment to get his neighborhood to join him. At every booth there has been an opportunity to involve oneself in an experiment of new or different service as part of one's Lenten discipline. As fair-goers finish their walk through the fairgrounds and prepare to go either home or to worship, all leave with a growing sense that many good things are coming not only out of Nazareth but their church, too. Many feel that they have met this Jesus and some even feel that they have been called to serve him. The Lenten season provides the context to follow on his path.

B. *Organization Of Event.*
1. Pre-event publicity and planning.
    a. Start planning and publicity in Advent if possible. Invitations, bulletin boards, newsletters, should be out or up no later then the beginning of Epiphany.
    b. Prepare a simple blank, dated Lenten calendar for each fair-goer. Blocks should be large enough so that notes can be written for commitments into the future.
    c. Ask all committees of the church and individual members to prepare a "display" of what they do in Christ's name both within the congregation and around the community. This can include pamphlets, display signs, and other information about their specific ministry. All standing committees should be expected to display within the Mission Fair.
    d. Identify and invite people from the congregation who work outside of the committee structure who are involved in such things as:
        1. Volunteering in a hospital.
        2. Recycling with the Boy Scouts.
        3. Delivering the altar flowers.
        4. Working in a Christian day care center.
    e. Ask the worship and music committee to coordinate sermon, music, and special prayers for the Mission Fair day.
    f. Be sure to provide nursery services for families with small children.
    g. Encourage all exhibitors to develop age-specific opportunities for service within their ministry area. Don't forget that children can help, too!

2. Getting the event together.
   a. Ask exhibitors to set up their booths throughout the building the day prior to the Mission Fair.
      1. Have lots of information.
      2. Have an inviting and exciting display.
      3. Have specific opportunities for service.
   b. Lay a paper footpath throughout the church. (A logical plan to move the people throughout the fair should be established.)
   c. Reserve space about halfway through the fair for a hospitality table.
   d. Place festive decorations throughout the building:
      1. Balloons.
      2. Banners.
      3. Posters.
      4. Any special lighting or music for the event.
   e. Supply greeters' stations with:
      1. Large welcoming poster.
      2. Name tags and pens.
      3. Lenten calendars.
      4. List and map of exhibitors.
3. Mission Fair morning.
   a. Greeters:
      1. Arrive at least a half hour early.
      2. Offer to help any exhibitors with last minute preparations.
      3. Welcome visitors with a smile, hand out materials and give directions to the nursery for those families with small children.
   b. Hospitality table is well set with coffee or tea, cold drinks and other refreshments as appropriate.

Section 1
Playlets

Introduction

1 — Lord, Everyone Is Searching For You
   Evangelism Playlet

2 — What Are They Doing To My Sabbath?
   Worship Playlet

3 — Can You See The Harvest?
   Education Ministries Playlet

4 — And They Cast Out Many Demons
   Social Concerns Playlet

5 — The Lord Of The Storm
   Stewardship Playlet

Introduction

In this chapter the *Come And See* resource continues with the invitation to have an inside look at the discipleship that happens within the committee structure of the congregation. What follows are five playlets in which members of church committees or councils struggle to be faithful disciples.

The themes for the playlets are evangelism, worship, education, social outreach and stewardship. The members of each committee are confronted with issues that test their faith and ask them to search earnestly for the gospel.

The playlets offer no easy answers or satisfactory resolutions. Rather, the aim is to invite the audience to reflect upon their own potential call to participate in one of these challenging ministries.

Each playlet is designed for five to six players and has a similar format: Three "committee members," and sometimes the pastor, meet around a table that can be set up in the sanctuary. The routine business for which they came together soon fades into the background as a troublesome issue claims their attention. Twice during the meeting their conversation is interrupted by shadowy figures who bring insight and clarification to the audience. However, the committee members cannot hear the people in the shadows. They have to search within themselves and with each other to find how God is present in their context.

Each playlet lasts approximately 10 minutes.

The playlets may be set within the context of a mid-week Lenten worship. The passages from the Gospel of Mark which form their basis are cited at the beginning of each section. These passages can be used as the Scripture readings during the service.

Hymn suggestions and prayers that ask God's continued blessing for the various ministries of the congregation have been included.

The introductory notes at the beginning of each playlet may be reproduced in worship bulletins.

It may be helpful to combine the worship event with a simple fellowship supper.

Those who wish to explore the various ministry themes further can use the Bible studies presented in the next section.

1 — Lord, Everyone Is Searching For You

A playlet about evangelism

1. **Scripture:** Mark 1:32-39

2. **Suggested Hymns:**
   Hark, the Voice of Jesus Calling
   Rise up, O Saints of God
   Lord, Speak to Us, That We May Speak

3. **Prayer:**
   Father in heaven, it is your will that all people may come to know the love you offer to us through your son Jesus Christ. In everything we do, inspire our witness to him. Teach us to share our faith at church, at work and at home. Guide and protect those in our congregation that diligently follow your call to make disciples of all peoples. Give them the power to speak your word so that every man, woman and child will live in the hope of the resurrection of our Lord Jesus Christ. We pray in his name. Amen.

4. **Introductory Notes:**
   In many churches, the pastor and the evangelism committee share the primary responsibilities for meeting, welcoming and incorporating the unchurched into the life of the congregation. All the baptized are called and empowered to bear witness to the love of God in the life, death and resurrection of Jesus Christ. Many Christians share their faith at school, work and around the neighborhoods where they live. This playlet focuses on the work of the evangelism committee as people come to worship seeking God's love. A small committee of very busy men and women tries to address some of the theological issues

and practical applications of being a welcoming people in the congregation.

The audience watches the committee at work. They see tension between the committee's ambiguity and its stated mission for evangelism. The playlet gives no clear answers or satisfactory resolutions to the "problem" that is presented. The audience is invited to discover what they can do to help those who are "searching for Jesus" come into relationship with Christ and His Body, the church.

5. Characters:

LARRY is the evangelism committee chairperson. He is a man of action. At this meeting he is tired because of his work schedule. He is frustrated by the apparent lack of connections between his committee work and his responsibility for evangelism.

JANET is a long-time member of the church. She seeks to gather all the facts and to include everyone and to be a peacemaker.

TED is a relatively new member of the congregation who loves to tell stories. He seems to gain insight and enthusiasm as he reflects on his own journey.

(LARRY, JANET and TED gather around a table set in the sanctuary and begin their conversation.)

LARRY: *(Tired and grumpy)* I almost didn't make it to this meeting of the evangelism committee tonight. I've been working overtime every day for weeks, and I just need to go home and get some rest.

JANET: I know what you mean. I have weeks, even months like that sometimes.

TED: Yes, and the worst thing about it is the guilt. My kids were saying I'm a great dad, it's just that I'm never around to play ball, or help with homework, or whatever.

LARRY: Well, it sounds like we all would like to be somewhere else. So, how about if we dispense with the minutes of our last meeting and get down to business right away. Janet, have you been able to line up any greeters for worship? I haven't been around for the last three weeks to see if you have.

JANET: I've really tried. But everyone I called said they'd feel "awkward" standing by the door glad-handing people as if they were strangers when Lord knows, we're family around here. If I had a penny for every time I heard the word "awkward" this past month we could actually afford those name tags for worship that the pastor keeps talking about. I guess those feelings are normal when you all feel like family.

TED: Yeah, that's what we like about this place. We like that we know everyone and most folks know us. Besides, if a stranger does come to church I know that someone will notice and say "Hi." Don't we trust in God and the Holy Spirit any more?

JANET: What do you mean, Ted?

TED: All of this evangelism stuff is getting me a little confused. Pastor always says that it is God who gives faith and that we should never feel smug about being here because it is God who brings us to church. So why does it seem up to us all of a sudden to make people feel good about being here? I thought that was up to the Holy Spirit.

JANET: Yes, I remember that sermon, too. Why is pastor asking us to do something that seems so unnecessary?

LARRY: You know it wasn't really the pastor's idea. We all went to that evangelism workshop and got excited about thinking of our church as a warm and welcoming place.

TED: But I think we already are, most of the time, anyway.

LARRY: Most of the time?

TED: Last month our daughter, Betsy, came to church early to get a good seat because I was going to help with worship. She wanted to be up close to see her daddy assist with the service for the first time. Well, she sat in Mr. Meyer's seat and he let her know in no uncertain terms that it was his seat and not hers!

LARRY: Everybody knows that Mr. Myers has been sitting in that seat for 20 years.

JANET: *(Laughs)* Sure, and that kind of stuff happens in every family. You didn't take it too seriously did you?

TED: No, but Betsy was crushed. She was embarrassed and thought she had done something terrible. All she really wanted was to cheer me on.

LARRY: *(Wearily)* Enough of the seating chart. Can we get back to the agenda? I'm really tired. Janet, I'll report to council that this business about the greeters is going slowly and we haven't found anyone yet. And now to new business. Pastor called just before the meeting tonight and said I should tell you that our third family has gone over to that new place.

TED: What new place, Larry? What are you talking about?

JANET: Well, if it's another family like the first two, I wouldn't be surprised.

TED: I still don't know what you're talking about.

LARRY: I can't believe you haven't heard about it, Ted. Even though I've been out of town for three weeks that is all they are talking about in my neighborhood. It seems that those people are going door to door . . . .

JANET: Oh! Those guys. They're part of that new fellowship thing down at the firehouse.

TED: You mean another church?

LARRY: Well, I'm not really sure that it's a church.

JANET: I don't know what they are exactly either. But I hear that the people who go there say it's really friendly and warm. That's why I think it's no surprise that those three families left. They were always saying how hard it was to get to know people around here . . . and how cliquish we were. I don't think that's true, but . . . .

TED: Well I don't think it's true either, but I still don't know what makes them so different from us.

LARRY: Ted, I'm not quite sure what's going on, but pastor told me on the phone that they had talked about that among the clergy the other day. Every new person who comes in the door at the firehouse gets some sort of guide that helps them through the service. And they send out cards and letters after their service, thanking people for coming.

JANET: Yeah, and my neighbor said that someone called her the day after she went and asked if she needed anything or if they could help her in some way. She was impressed.

LARRY: Anyway, Ted, it's a lot of gimmicks. And people are falling for it. At least I think it's just gimmicks. I haven't heard anybody say anything about the gospel or truth or what church is all about. And I don't quite understand what pastor wants us to do. We're the evangelism committee, not some group that warns our congregation against gimmicks.

(A person steps out of the shadows and reads the following letter to the audience.)

Dear Pastor,

My wife, Mary, told me that you called the other day while I was at work. As newcomers to the community, we're really glad you offered to set up an appointment to visit with us about our Christian faith and church membership. We also really appreciated your sermon this past Sunday when we came to worship at your church. It was obvious to us that you are a woman of great faith and you speak from your heart when you preach.

But, as important as your concern and good preaching were for us, we don't want to waste your time any further.

My wife and I have decided to continue looking for a church home that might be more open to strangers like us. It was obvious that everyone in your congregation cared a great deal for one another, but we felt like intruders at a family reunion. No one was mean or nasty or even cold. It's just that we felt like we were bothering the ushers when we had to ask for a bulletin and directions to the nursery. The same was true at the coffee hour after the service. My wife and I are shy people and didn't want to impose on your congregation's fellowship. I guess our shyness might be our problem and not your congregation's, but our feelings of awkwardness really distracted us from hearing God's message. We hope to find a church where we are made to feel at home in Christ's name and where we can help others feel that way, too.

Thanks again for a good sermon and your personal interest and concern.

Sincerely, Henry Andersen

(The conversation at the table resumes.)

TED: Well, wait a minute. Maybe there are some important connections between those gimmicks and evangelism.

LARRY: Like what?

TED: Now I think this congregation is warm and loving. But when Joyce and I came to town it was a different story.

JANET: How was it different? We've always been family.

TED: No, those people who left our congregation do have a point. I think we can be an intimidating bunch — at least at first glance. I remember our first Sunday. About three weeks after we had moved here, we finally decided to look for a church home. I had driven by this church a number of times but could not see a time for the church service.

JANET: You mean there wasn't a sign out there?

TED: Oh, yes, there was a sign, but I couldn't see the time when service started, and I couldn't find it in the yellow pages either.

LARRY: I'm glad we've changed our church sign. At least that makes sense to me. Now anyone searching for a church home can immediately see the time for worship.

TED: Anyhow, it wasn't so then. I figured every church starts at 11 o'clock.

LARRY: *(Wearily)* Good guess, Ted.

TED: We didn't want to take a chance on being late so we got here at quarter of. The kids were irritable, you know how kids are. Betsy was just a baby and our teenager was griping about being bored and didn't want to look foolish being seen going to church with her parents.

JANET: Our kids don't want to be seen with us anywhere either. I know what you mean.

TED: Well, our teenager didn't have anything to worry about. Nobody noticed us coming in the door. The ushers were too busy talking to each other to see us.

JANET: That sounds a little harsh, Ted. They were probably getting last minute instructions or something else really important.

TED: I don't mean to be harsh. I'm just describing what happened.

JANET: Well, I know my Ralph is there every Sunday. He tries real hard to talk with everyone and . . . .

LARRY: Oh, come on! You're sounding like a bunch of school children. Just get on with your story so we can get to the point and go home.

TED: We decided not to look for the nursery so we took Betsy into worship with us. Talk about a mistake. Halfway into the prelude I realized that we didn't have a bulletin. So I got up to find an usher and that's when Betsy started to scream. I didn't think she'd ever stop. People were staring, our teenager wanted to crawl under the pew. By the end of the service we were all exhausted and just wanted to get out of there. When we got home we agreed that we were too embarrassed to come back — ever!

JANET: Something obviously changed your mind. What happened? Was it a call from the pastor?

TED: Well, the pastor did call. She said she had noticed us. I'm sure she did. I'm sure that the entire congregation had noticed us by that time. I know that pastor was trying to be nice but that just made us feel worse.

LARRY: Well then, what brought you back?

TED: Chocolate chip cookies.

LARRY: *(Irritated)* Come on, Ted. That sounds just like the gimmicks they're using over at the firehouse.

TED: I'm serious. That Wednesday night John and Elizabeth showed up at our door with a box of chocolate chip cookies. They said they just wanted to make us feel welcome. They told us about their first Sunday in church with their baby. We swapped stories about kids and work and other things for an hour or more. And then, before they left, Elizabeth said that she would help Joyce with Betsy when we came to church the following Sunday.

JANET: See, I told you we were family. Some people here went out of their way to welcome you!

TED: We really felt the love of Christ in their friendly witness. And besides that, it was Elizabeth's chocolate chip cookies that are responsible for me being a member of this committee.

LARRY: Sure.

TED: Really! I was eating some more chocolate chip cookies when you asked me to serve on the evangelism committee. I remembered their visit and just couldn't say no to you.

LARRY: Well, I'm really glad that you're here, but, I would like to get back to the agenda. So what are we supposed to tell the pastor?

TED: *(With new insight)* Maybe that we'll think about those gimmicks some more. If everyone in this place were more like John and Elizabeth . . . .

JANET: But John and Elizabeth aren't gimmicks!

TED: You're right. But everything they did made it clear to us that church is a place where love is given to everyone, including those who come with screaming babies and aren't members.

LARRY: But isn't there a way to show that love other than in guides and cookies and letters and cards?

(A person steps out of the shadows and reads the following letter to the audience.)

Dear Pastor,

I've just moved into your community. One of my best friends from college told me that he used to be a member at your church. He said that it was a real close-knit family of faith. Although I haven't been active in church as an adult, I am searching for that love of God that Christians always seem to talk about. My friend says that I will surely find it at your church.

I hope to see you this Sunday at worship and will set up an appointment with you to discuss church membership.

Sincerely, Tom Brown

2 — What Are They Doing To My Sabbath?

A playlet about worship

1. **Scripture:** Mark 2:23-28

2. **Suggested Hymns:**
   Where Charity and Love Prevail
   The Church of Christ, in Every Age
   In Christ There Is No East or West

3. **Prayer:**
   Almighty God, whom the saints delight to worship in heaven and on earth: As we come into your presence fill us with joy and thanksgiving for the gift of your word of forgiveness and hope. Open our hearts and minds so that our congregation will be a place where all people can worship in justice and truth. Bless the ministry of those who serve as worship leaders in this congregation. Allow them to work diligently and faithfully so that your name will be glorified in all the earth. This we pray in Jesus' name. Amen.

4. **Introductory Notes:**
   In many congregations there is a group of men and women who help the pastor plan and organize the worship life of the church. Responsibilities vary from place to place and can include such things as ensuring that the sanctuary is ready on Sunday morning, that lay worship leaders are properly trained, and that the worship life is planned according to the season of the church year. All the baptized who come to worship each Sunday bring certain assumptions and feelings about what should happen. Some Christians cherish a good choir and rousing hymns. Others yearn for the traditions of their youth, and

still others are particular about the sermon. This playlet focuses on the work of the worship committee and pastor as the congregation finds itself in the midst of a struggle over the "right way" to worship. New people from the immediate neighborhood have joined or want to join the congregation. However, these newcomers are primarily people of Hispanic origin and have some problems understanding an all-English liturgy. The audience for this playlet is invited to struggle with the worship committee as the committee tries to redefine the vision and mission of this congregation.

5. **Characters:**
MILDRED is the worship chairperson. She is a long-time member and has a strong faith. This allows her to trust God and be open to change. At this meeting she is discouraged because the church council, i.e., the administrative body of the church, has voted against the committee's proposals.

FRANCES is a member of the committee who likes the congregation's worship life just the way it is. She sees herself as the spokesperson for nameless others who share her views.

BOB, a member of the committee, has many friends in the Hispanic community and hopes that the congregation will minister to them. He is an advocate for their concerns.

THE PASTOR is a proponent of inclusive ministry but is sometimes ineffective and politically unwise as a change agent.

(MILDRED, FRANCES, BOB and PASTOR gather around a table set in the sanctuary and begin their conversation.)

MILDRED: Pastor, I'm glad you came tonight. I am so discouraged about what happened at the council meeting the other night.

PASTOR: I'm discouraged, too. I guess I should have delayed my vacation until we had this situation ironed out.

BOB: Wait a minute! I was out of town last week. Would somebody please bring me up to date?

MILDRED: Sorry. I just couldn't bring myself to call you. Every one of the changes we proposed to council got shot down! Every one of them! There will be no 8:30 Spanish language service. We even had some rather heated discussion about all of the liturgical changes that we have already made. The Worship Committee sure took a beating this time.

FRANCES: I told you we were moving much too fast. This congregation just isn't ready for one of the Sunday morning services to be in Spanish. I'm not either. I went along with you on the recommendation to include some Spanish hymns, but this is too much too fast.

BOB: You mean they said no to everything? Mildred, did you tell them then about what happened when I brought my neighbor Jose and his parents to worship?

MILDRED: I tried to.

BOB: That was really awkward. I thought they were doing great following the service. But on the way home in the car, I realized that they had barely understood a word of the sermon.

MILDRED: I really did the best I could, Bob.

BOB: I didn't mean to say that you hadn't tried. It's just that when this proposal came up I got so excited that I went right over to tell Jose and his folks. Now I feel like a fool.

FRANCES: Serves you right for speaking out before the council votes on something as important as this.

BOB: Frances, you're right. It is important. That's why I spoke out. I really thought that we wanted to follow Jesus into our neighborhoods and feed his flock. But I guess the council didn't see it that way.

PASTOR: I wasn't there. Mildred, what did happen anyway?

MILDRED: Well, Pastor, I'd say that most of the folks on council had heard about our proposals before I even had a chance to give my report. And a lot of them had made up their minds. As a matter of fact I thought they were downright nasty.

FRANCES: Oh, Mildred, you're exaggerating. I was there and I think they dealt with the issues.

PASTOR: What do you think the issues are, or were?

FRANCES: Are we a Lutheran (substitute any denomination here) church or what? You shouldn't mess around with hundreds of years of tradition. Of course people are going to be upset. Three years ago you made us get those new hymnals. Next, we had to have communion every Sunday. You even changed the language of the Lord's Prayer. We're tired of all these changes.

PASTOR: But Frances, our worship life is always changing because we are always changing. We don't say the Lord's Prayer in Greek or German anymore. Traditions are only good if they help us hear God's word clearly. As a matter of fact, this denomination was founded by a man who broke with hundreds of years of tradition in favor of the gospel.

FRANCES: Yes, but that was about indulgences and the Pope and purgatory. You wanted to change the language of our service. Luther didn't do that.

BOB: Frances, you're wrong. We just went through this in the adult Sunday school class. Luther did change the language of the Mass from Latin to German so people could understand the gospel.

PASTOR: For that matter it started with the apostles and the Holy Spirit at Pentecost. Remember how the people were gathered at the temple and they all heard about the mighty acts of God in their own language.

FRANCES: I understand all of that, but why do we have to do it? I thought that's what the Catholic church down the street was doing.

MILDRED: As a matter of fact, that's how the council justified their vote to keep all of our services as they are right now. The Catholic church does have a mass in Spanish.

(A person steps out of the shadows and reads the following letter to the audience.)

Dear Council President,

I want to express my heartfelt appreciation for your work in leading the council to the right decision about this Spanish worship service. I have been a member of this church for 30 years, even though the neighborhood changed and I am 20 miles out in the suburbs now. What brings me back to this place Sunday after Sunday is the familiarity and constancy of our worship life. I know what to expect when I walk into the sanctuary on Sunday and so does everyone else. Church just wouldn't be the same without the traditions we all cherish so much.

I know we should minister to the Spanish people around the church but I'm glad we didn't choose our worship life as the place to start. Maybe we could have an after school program for them, to teach them English. Wouldn't this be a great way to help them into our culture? Then maybe they could appreciate this great heritage of ours as much as I do.

Again, my sincere thanks for doing the right thing.

In Christ, Hans Krenz

(The conversation at the table resumes.)

BOB: But all of my neighbors aren't Roman Catholic and those who aren't Catholic are looking for a church home just like the rest of us. We have no right to deny them God's word by saying that someone else could or should do it.

FRANCES: The council isn't denying anyone anything. God's word is proclaimed in the sanctuary every Sunday in English. If anyone wants to, he can come and hear it.

PASTOR: But that's the problem. They can't hear it because so many don't speak English. That's what Bob was trying to tell us about Jose and his family. To have only English services in this neighborhood is like giving a hungry person a can of food without an opener. Mildred, I'm really sorry I wasn't at council to help talk about this.

FRANCES: Pastor, you're getting too dramatic about this. I said from the start that I was in favor of some Spanish hymns or anthems, even a prayer now and then — to help us all get used to them. We just tried to move too far, too fast with a full Spanish service. Where would our 8:30 people go for their worship service? *(Pause)* You know it's not just the Spanish thing, there are still a lot of our folks who don't like the new Lord's Prayer.

BOB: It sounds like we're worshiping tradition rather than God around here.

MILDRED: Bob, I think you're right. But, where do we go from here?

PASTOR: Maybe the first thing we've got to realize is that it's not "us" versus "them." Jesus is Lord of all people and he's even Lord of the traditions that many of our members hold so dear.

FRANCES: That's what I've been saying all along.

PASTOR: *(With laughing frustration)* Frances, I think you still misunderstand. You've been trying to care for our members which is a wonderful thing, but not enough for Christians. Jesus asks us to care for everyone — even if it means having to give up what we love so very much.

MILDRED: Amen, Pastor, and I'm not willing to give up just yet.

(A person steps out of the shadows and reads the following letter.)

Dear Pastor,

In reviewing recent census data we've discovered that St. John's is one of a growing number of churches in predominantly Hispanic neighborhoods. Several seminaries have approached us to develop appropriate training sites for interns of Hispanic origin.

Our cross-cultural ministry representative, Pastor Juanita Gomez, is eager to visit you and your people and review your programs with the Hispanic community. We are especially interested in congregations that offer bilingual worship services and programs that identify and celebrate the richness and diversity of the Hispanic traditions.

Please arrange a meeting for Pastor Gomez with as many of your Anglo and Hispanic leaders as possible. May the Lord of the church bless you in your cross-cultural ministry.

In Christ, Pastor Hofzinger

3 — Can You See The Harvest?

A playlet about educational ministries

1. Scripture: Mark 4:26-29

2. Suggested Hymns:
Almighty God, Your Word is Cast
God Moves in a Mysterious Way
If You But Trust in God to Guide You

3. Prayer:
Lord God, you are our source of wisdom and knowledge. Help us to study your word diligently so that we may grow in your love and in all that is good. Bless and support all who teach and all who learn that together we may grow in faith and service to you. We pray in Jesus' name. Amen.

4. Introductory Notes:
One of the most vital concerns of any congregation is its educational program. Together with worship, the teaching ministries of the church are central in congregational life. Many churches have important committees which oversee the curriculum and administration of the various educational programs. Those whose discipleship has led them to participate in this ministry know of the struggles that churches face in this area. Issues often revolve around whether classes are interesting enough to keep attendance up; whether programs adequately address current crises facing Christians; and whether programs are faithful to the witness of the gospel.

This playlet focuses on the work of the education committee as they discuss an aspect of the youth ministry of the church. The members of the committee feel caught between the unrealistic expectations of parents and their own desire to serve God in a faithful manner. The audience is invited to share in their struggle and to discover what they can do to help those who teach and educate.

5. Characters:

DAVE is the chairperson of the committee. He is also a council member and he sees himself under attack from parents. He acutely feels the lack of support from those who can only criticize and even from members of his committee.

SARA is a teacher in the church school. She has been teaching for three years. For her, discipleship is simply a matter of ethics. She sees involvement not as a gift from God but as her duty to her own children.

CHUCK is a teacher of ninth grade confirmands. He has just rejoined the church after a long absence and is still tentative about the work of the committee itself but fired up by the joy of the gospel to teach young people. His personal struggle is to understand what brought him back to church and how God is working in his life.

(DAVE, SARA and CHUCK gather around a table set with four chairs and begin their conversation.)

DAVE: Well, it's 20 minutes before eight and Margaret is not here. Let's get started with this evaluation meeting for the confirmation retreat. Sara, I believe you have devotions for tonight.

SARA: Yes, Dave, I do. It's not much, but I think it's relevant to what we're doing. I want to read these verses from Mark: "And he said, 'The kingdom of God is as if a man should scatter seed upon the ground, and should sleep and rise night and day, and the seed should sprout and grow, he knows not how. The earth produces itself, first the blade, then the ear, then the full grain in the ear. But when the grain is ripe, at once he puts in the sickle, because the harvest has come.' " To me this parable has always meant that we should sow seeds of learning about God so that our kids grow up to be faithful Christians. We all know that the youth are the future of our church. That is why this story came to mind for tonight.

DAVE: Thanks, Sara. Let's get on with the evaluation. Chuck, could you give us a summary of the kids' written evaluations from the end of the retreat?

CHUCK: I've compiled what I have, but only about half of the kids turned them in. Margaret was going to talk with the other retreat leaders, but she's not here.

SARA: How can we ever do the right thing if we don't have the information? We'll never get a good confirmation program at this rate.

CHUCK: Wait a minute. Let me tell you what I do have. Some of it seems pretty good. Most of the kids who gave me their evaluations said the retreat was very helpful. They said that this was the first time they got to talk about sexuality and their values. At school they just talk about "doing it." But pastor and the rest of us helped them talk about feelings, and peer pressure, and awkwardness.

DAVE: Well, I'm glad to hear we've had at least one positive thing happening around that retreat. I've been getting nothing but grief since the day we said this retreat was mandatory for all ninth graders.

SARA: What kind of grief, Dave? I thought all of these parents wanted their kids confirmed. Confirmation has certain requirements. They will just have to understand that.

DAVE: Easier said than done.

CHUCK: What do you mean?

DAVE: You don't have to put up with all those disgruntled parents every Sunday. I can't even go to get a cup of coffee at the fellowship hour without getting attacked.

CHUCK: Oh, Dave, you're exaggerating!

DAVE: *(Angry)* You know what I went through for this retreat? Lots of parents said they didn't know why we had to go so far away for a retreat when we could have had a lock-in at the church like we did for Halloween. Then there were the ones who didn't see what sex and confirmation had to do with one another. And there were lots who said we had ruined their weekend plans because of all the homework you give the kids each week.

CHUCK: *(In disbelief)* Homework? I told them to flip through the magazines at home and to cut out advertising pictures that used sexuality to promote a product. Some of the kids thought it was a neat idea.

SARA: What did that have to do with the retreat?

CHUCK: We made a montage to see what messages society gives us about sex. Then we looked in the Bible for what it says about sexuality.

SARA: I guess that's one way to get kids to read their Bible. That's pretty tricky, Chuck. I could try something like that in my class.

CHUCK: No. The pictures were as important as the Bible. All I wanted was for the kids to learn something about themselves.

DAVE: I'm glad that you two are swapping teaching techniques, but we're here to evaluate the retreat. I'm really tired of taking all this myself and there will be even more at the parents' meeting next week. Chuck, I know you will be there, but I'm just exhausted. Sara, will you go in my place if we work out the details tonight?

SARA: No way! I won't go in your place! It's tough enough teaching my class and serving on this committee. I only do it because it's my duty to my children. You're the chairperson, you're supposed to do this.

CHUCK: I'll go, but I won't put up with a lot of criticism. As far as I'm concerned, it was a great retreat. Ask the kids.

DAVE: The kids aren't the issue. The parents are, and I'm tired of beating my head against the wall — alone! No matter what we do, people gripe. It never goes anywhere anyway. Who gets into a good college because they're a confirmed member of St. John's church anyhow?

CHUCK: *(Emphatic)* The kids are the issue, Dave. Confirmation is trying to prepare our young people for a full life with God and his church. It's not about catering to the parents.

SARA: Chuck is right, Dave. We have to teach our kids about morality and God because nobody else will.

(A person steps out of the shadows and reads the following letter to the audience.)

Dear Pastor,

The college that I'm applying to has asked for a number of personal references. My parents said I should ask you to write one for me. It would help a lot since you know me pretty well. The director of admissions said she would send you the form.

Getting ready for college has really made me think about a lot of things. Grades are real important and so is my boyfriend. I can even see that the church has been important. I have to admit that I didn't always want to go to Sunday school and church. By the time I started confirmation, church was a big yawn, but my parents made me go.

Funny thing, though, I learned some important stuff. There were many times when I was confused and didn't know who I was or what I was doing. At those times it was important to think that no matter who I was, God was the same. I guess I still don't have it all together about God and me and my future, but those years in church helped me understand that God and I can talk and listen to one another. Some of my friends still think they have to do it all alone, by themselves. I feel sorry for them.

I especially want to say thanks for all the retreats we went on. The one on sexuality in particular helped me learn a lot about myself. It has been three years but I still remember your openness to all of our questions. It wasn't that you or any of the leaders tried to give us answers. You simply helped us discover new ways to think about ourselves in relationships with friends and with God.

Thank you very much for everything,
Jenny

(The conversation at the table resumes.)

DAVE: *(Sarcastically)* I'm glad you can see your teaching task so clearly. I've had it. I've been doing this for three years and there is nothing but complaints. And what good does it do anyway? No matter what we do, no matter how good our programs are, as soon as these kids are confirmed they're out the door and never come back. All the griping by the parents and all of our improvements won't make a difference. I'm ready to quit. Even you two won't give me any help and Margaret is never here.

CHUCK: Now wait a minute, Dave. I know that I'm new to this committee. I've only been on it for six months and I don't have to put up with the complaints like you do, but let me tell you why I'm here and why I'm going to stay.

DAVE: Chuck, you don't have to try to talk me out of this. This is something that I've been thinking about for a long time. I just feel like I'm always running in circles or putting out brush fires with parents.

CHUCK: If that is what Christian education were all about, I would feel that way, too. But, when Sara read from Mark tonight I heard something that she didn't say.

SARA: All I said was that if we want a harvest, we have to plant the seed. If we want our kids to be straight and believe in God, we have to teach every day.

CHUCK: We do have to teach them, Sara, but there aren't any guarantees. We don't know if they're going to listen or respond or grow up right — whatever that means. Look at me. I was raised in the church, confirmed with the other teenagers and then disappeared until about a year ago when Meghan was born.

SARA: Well, you were one of the lucky ones. Maybe your church's programs weren't as good as ours. I certainly hope that my children never leave the church. That's why I'm working so hard. I'm glad you're back, but you never should have left in the first place.

CHUCK: Well, I don't know if I chose to leave or simply drifted away. And to tell the truth, I don't even know why I'm back. Somehow it seems like the decision to come back wasn't up to me.

DAVE: Of course not. Everybody comes back to church to get married and then when they want their babies baptized.

CHUCK: No. That's not it for me. Meghan's baptism may have brought me back, but look at me. I'm teaching confirmation and I'm having a great time doing it. I look forward to those kids and their questions. This has got to be a gift from God. And that's what I thought about when you read from Mark, Sara. I don't understand how it grew, but I'm convinced that God has given me this harvest of joy. That's why I'm sticking around.

(A person steps out of the shadows and reads the following letter to the congregation.)

Dear Pastor,

Please remove our family's name from the membership rolls of St. John's church. Since our daughter, Kathy, got pregnant we have come to realize how little this church has done to help Kathy grow up right and to prevent this tragedy. We always taught her that she should learn the difference between right and wrong in Sunday school and all of those retreats. We always did everything you asked us to do for her religious upbringing. But, what did it get us? A pregnant 17-year-old. A baby having a baby.

If this is the best that this church can do, God help us all.
The Jones Family

(The conversation at the table resumes.)

CHUCK: We are responsible for one another. That's what sowing the seed is all about. That's why you have to stay on this committee, Dave. It's important. But you don't have to go crazy worrying about the harvest, about the results. That's up to God.

5 — And They Cast Out Many Demons

A playlet about social concerns ministries

1. Scripture: Mark 6:7-13

2. Suggested Hymns:
Lord, Whose Love in Humble Service
O Master, Let Me Walk With You
There's a Wideness in God's Mercy

3. Prayer:
God of love and compassion, your Son came to heal the sick and to cast out demons. Open our hearts and minds to those who live with injustice, terror, disease and death as their constant companions. Help us eliminate the power of evil and oppression. Uphold the men and women in our congregation whose call it is to serve those who have none to care for them. Strengthen all care-givers in their faith. Give them the power to heal what is broken in body and spirit. We pray in the name of the greatest healer of all, your Son, Jesus Christ our Lord. Amen.

4. Introductory Notes:
Jesus calls us to love, serve and care for our neighbors. Sometimes this call to love the neighbor is difficult to follow — particularly when the neighbor is not one of our own. We use money as a barrier between us and those undesirables whom we do not wish to see or touch or even have in the same room with us. It is so much easier to give a contribution to some worthwhile organization than to face the possibility of having to come in close contact with people we fear.

This playlet focuses on the social concerns group of a congregation. The members in this group have to face the difficult decision of whether or not to let an AIDS support group use the church building. The playlet gives no answers. It does show that such neighborliness always involves an intense soul-searching to determine what is most faithful to the call of Christ. The audience is invited to ask itself how it would react to such a request. What fears and prejudices make us lose sight of Jesus' call to love the neighbor?

5. **Characters:**
SCOTT is the chairperson of the committee. He has placed the support group's request on the committee's agenda. He is unprepared for the surprises and revelations that occur during the meeting.

MARY is quiet and reserved. There are many things that the committee does not know about her. She tries to live out her discipleship through hands-on experience. Through her, the audience learns something about the suffering and pain that AIDS victims and their families have to endure.

RUTH is a young professional with a small child in the church's nursery school. She is very active in the social programs of the church. However, the prospects of her child coming in contact with AIDS is too frightening for her to contemplate.

(SCOTT, MARY and RUTH gather around a table set in the sanctuary and begin their conversation.)

SCOTT: Thanks for coming together on this rainy night. I hope all of you got the minutes from last time so you know what's on the agenda. I'd like to begin with a short prayer: "Lord Jesus, you came to save the lost. Help us, your disciples, to recognize the lost in our time. Give us the grace to minister to them now even as you did then. Amen." Are we ready to begin? *(All nod affirmation)* Okay. Mary, why don't you start by telling us how the food pantry is doing?

MARY: The volunteers tell me that we had 60 families come for help last month. We're kind of low on baby food but the scouts really helped with lots of canned goods.

SCOTT: Do you think an announcement about the shortage in the bulletin would be helpful?

MARY: We could do that. But we're always asking for so much! Can we just use some of the committee money until the stock is replenished in some other way?

SCOTT: Ruth, what do our finances look like?

RUTH: Our finances are fine. We could do either or both. If the babies need food let's just get it. *(Pause. Obviously impatient.)* I know there is still a lot of other business, but I really want to talk about the request from the AIDS group.

SCOTT: The AIDS request is on the agenda for tonight, Ruth. But we really ought to decide how to get the baby food. And there are a couple of other things that we ought to get out of the way first.

RUTH: Scott, we can always work out the details of those other things. We have got to talk about this AIDS group right away. George and I really got into this at dinner tonight and we're scared.

SCOTT: *(Startled by her intensity)* Ruth, you're usually as professional here as I've seen you at the office. Where is all of this anxiety coming from? We'll get to the AIDS group request.

RUTH: When I picked up Amanda from nursery school this afternoon, the teachers and all the parents were buzzing about this AIDS thing. Everybody knows about it. And everybody is scared!

MARY: Scared about what?

RUTH: Scared that this group of people with AIDS is going to meet downstairs on Wednesday nights. Scott told us that last month just as we were getting ready to leave.

MARY: I know. But I don't know why that should have everyone buzzing. Do they think these people are immoral?

RUTH: Well it's obvious, isn't it? They're really afraid that their children might get AIDS. *(Pause)* They want to use the nursery rooms for the meetings.

SCOTT: Wait a minute. Nothing has been decided. Nobody had been given permission to meet anywhere. The request is on our agenda for the first time tonight.

RUTH: It may be the first official time to talk about it but everybody knows and everybody is scared.

MARY: Instead of all this fear, I wish we could have some AIDS education around here. There really isn't anything for those parents to be afraid of.

RUTH: Easy for you to say. Your kids aren't in the nursery school program.

MARY: No. But I've been an AIDS volunteer with hospice for the past six months and I've learned a lot of things about AIDS.

SCOTT: Gee, I didn't know you were working with hospice. I guess there are a lot of things I still don't know about you. You're so quiet most of the time.

RUTH: I bet one of the things you learned at hospice is that everyone, everyone, with AIDS dies. *(Pause — softens)* That's why they're afraid for their children. Nobody wants to see their children die.

MARY: *(Softly)* I know. *(Pause)* It's been a year and a half since my brother, Mark, died. *(Long pause, wistfully)* AIDS is what killed him.

(A person steps out of the shadows and reads the following letter to the audience.)

Dear Pastor Ralph,
My husband and I wanted to send you this picture of our son Gregg. You can see from the picture that he was a big, strong, happy kid. We wanted you to have this because you never got to see him healthy and full of life. We can't thank you enough for the love and care and hope that you brought to all of us. We didn't know where to turn or what to do when our beautiful son came home to tell us that he was dying of AIDS. Our whole world collapsed. You know how isolated, and ashamed and alone we felt. It was only you and the people from hospice who saw us through this nightmare. All of you brought the love of God into our pain. It helped us realize that we were not alone. More important, Gregg knew that God still loved him. You really helped turn all of his doubts around. Please keep us in your prayers.
Margaret Olson

(The conversation at the table resumes.)

SCOTT: I'm sorry, Mary, I guess I didn't know your brother died of AIDS.

RUTH: I certainly didn't know that, either. I'm sorry, too. *(Pause)* Then I guess you really know what I'm talking about. I don't know what I'd do if my Amanda got AIDS. And the other parents feel the same way.

MARY: Ruth, you can't get the virus just by using the same room. My parents and I took care of Mark at home for three months. None of us has tested positive.

RUTH: Maybe you were lucky. I just don't want to take any chances.

MARY: It's not a matter of chance.

SCOTT: I agree with Mary. The disease is not communicated by casual contact. People have to do very specific things to transmit the virus.

MARY: There is probably a lot that we could all learn about AIDS . . . and we should. But, beyond that, we have been asked to help people who are sick and dying. That's what Jesus sends us out to do, isn't it?

RUTH: Mary, of course you are right. George and I joined this church because it has a reputation for outreach with the food pantry and the nursery school. But with this issue I'm just too afraid.

MARY: And Jesus has empowered his followers to cast out demons, too. Usually, I'm very quiet, but on this issue we have got to speak out and cast out these demons of ignorance and fear. People are dying, and we're just standing by, doing nothing.

(A person steps out of the shadows and reads the following letter to the audience.)

Dear Ralph:
 I tried to call your office before I went on vacation but couldn't reach you there. Things really got out of hand at St. John's and I had to let you know before you got caught up in it. Two months ago the AIDS support network approached our church leaders hoping to find a place to hold their weekly group meetings. As you know, we're pretty conservative. I thought the request would simply be denied. Boy, was I wrong. I haven't seen such a floor fight in years. There was fear,

self-righteousness and anger everywhere. People took sides and wouldn't budge. Some of our members are still so hot that they can barely sit together for worship. We both know that the AIDS group needs our support. But it has caused terrible conflict here. We did finally turn them down. They still need a place and I heard a rumor that they want to talk with you next. I don't want to tell you what to do. I just want to let you know what happened at my church. No matter what you do at your place, you're probably in for a big fight. God be with you. We'll talk when I get back from vacation.
Bill

(The conversation at the table resumes.)

SCOTT: I really think that this issue is too big for the three of us to handle.

RUTH: No, it's not! *(Turning to Mary)* I'm sorry but the parents just don't want them in our church.

MARY: The parents don't set the policy for the church, Jesus does.

SCOTT: *(Reluctantly)* Well, sort of. We at least need to know what the rest of the church leaders have to say. Let's pass it on to the council and inform pastor Ralph.

5 — The Lord Of The Storm

A playlet about stewardship

1. **Scripture:** Mark 4:35-41

2. **Suggested Hymns:**
   God Moves in a Mysterious Way
   Jesus Calls Us, O'er the Tumult
   Take My Life, That I Might Be

3. **Prayer:**
   Almighty God, creator of heaven and earth: All that we have is from your bountiful hands. Draw our minds to you, fill our imaginations and give us the will to care for all that you have entrusted to us. Let no one abuse the precious resources of your creation and guide us to be good stewards. Bless especially those who serve you as stewards in this congregation. Give them the patience to speak your word diligently and move all to respond in gratitude to your gracious goodness. We ask this in the name of Jesus, our Lord. Amen.

4. **Introductory Notes:**
   In recent years many congregations have broadened their stewardship focus to include the care of our communities, the environment, and the preservation of precious resources. God, the creator of all things, calls us to honor what we have received from his loving hand. Many Christians try to live out their discipleship by being advocates for the environment and by speaking out against abuse and neglect.
   This playlet focuses on the work of the stewardship committee and pastor. The people on this committee are called to balance the need of a community concern to end pollution at a factory with the suffering this may cause for those who will lose their jobs as a result. There is tension between those

whose entire livelihood is threatened and those who see the abuse of the environment as signaling the end of the planet. The audience is invited to explore the idea that stewardship is more than simply raising funds for the church. They are invited to ask whether the call from God to be good stewards is something that moves the people of the church beyond the congregation and into the world.

5. Characters:

LINDA is the stewardship chairperson. At first her vision of the task is somewhat limited to the congregation. She has enough on her hands just trying to balance the church's budget.

HANK is a production line worker at the plant that might shut its doors because it cannot meet pollution control standards. He is fearful, angry and confused.

PAUL has joined this committee because he sees himself as an environmental advocate. For him, stewardship is concern for the earth. His focus has blinded him to some of the suffering the plant shutdown may cause.

THE PASTOR is not always present for committee meetings but he has come this time because of pastoral concerns. He seeks help and information from committee members.

(LINDA, HANK, PAUL and PASTOR gather around a table set in the sanctuary. A person steps out of the shadows and reads the following newspaper article to the audience.)

THE PATRIOT NEWS ... EPA Threatens to Close United

Centerville, April 20. The Environmental Protection Agency (EPA) said it is prepared to close the United Plastics plant unless it receives detailed assurances showing how the company will implement new pollution controls.

The company has been charged with a large number of violations because existing controls do not meet current federal and state regulations. United, which has operated its plant in this area for 40 years, met with EPA officials and town leaders yesterday. A spokesman for the company said that declining profits in the last five years along with the need for more modern pollution safeguards may require the company to shut down its operation in Centerville. Workers at United, the largest employer in the region, were contacted for comment. Most said that they feared for their jobs. Last year United was repeatedly picketed by environmental groups. Pressure from these groups brought on the current action by the EPA.

(The conversation at the table begins.)

LINDA: Pastor, I'm surprised to see you here tonight. I always appreciate your help in the fall with our stewardship campaign. Is there something important that you want to talk with us about?

PASTOR: As a matter of fact, there is. Did all of you see the article in today's paper about United?

(All nod or acknowledge in the affirmative.)

PASTOR: The reporter wants to do a follow-up story on community reaction to United's problem. He called me this afternoon to see what area pastors think about it. I told him that I think this is a stewardship issue, and that I'd like to talk with my committee about it first.

LINDA: Stewardship issue? Oh, you mean because we might lose some members if they close the plant?

PAUL: No, that's not it. I understand why pastor is here. As Christians we're called to be good stewards of the earth. We have to speak out against them polluting the earth.

PASTOR: Well, to me the issue is a little more complicated than that. We do need to consider what will happen to this community if the plant closes.

LINDA: Pastor, you're probably right about the issues, but shouldn't you be talking to the social ministry committee?

PASTOR: No, Linda, this really is the group to talk with . . . .

LINDA: *(Interrupts)* Hey, look, we're a small committee and we still have our hands full trying to get people to give to this church. You know that the pledging program needs a lot of follow-up. We're just now starting to get on top of it.

PAUL: Well, I for one, am glad you brought this concern to us. The reason I volunteered here is because I feel that stewardship is more than just giving 10 percent to the church. I'm trying to teach the church that everything that we have is God's and what we do with it is stewardship. Nobody should have the right to pollute God's earth. We should say so loud and clear.

HANK: *(Explodes)* I'll tell you about my "loud and clear." The fear wakes me up in the night with visions of what my family's life is going to be like if United shuts down. Let me tell you "loud and clear" that we don't have enough savings to last three months. Every time I look at the kids I get back a message "loud and clear" that they don't have a chance of college or anything if United shuts down. And I'll tell you something else "loud and clear," this isn't an issue! What this is is my life, and lots of others. You're talking like I'm not even in the room.

(Stunned silence and jittery movement)

PASTOR: I never meant to make light of this or keep it at a distance, Hank. One of the reasons I came here tonight is because it is so important and so heart-wrenching. No matter what happens, a lot of people will be hurt. I need to find out how I can best help.

HANK: One of the ways to help is to understand that I'm dealing with this differently than you guys are. The rumors have been around for weeks and the story hit the paper this morning but not one of you said, "I'm sorry," or asked how this might affect me and my family.

(Stunned silence again)

PAUL: Wait a minute, Hank. You're right. When I heard the rumors I did think about you and some of the others in this congregation. I just didn't want to pry.

LINDA: Me either. I understand how you feel.

HANK: No, I don't think you do. Do you guys realize what a shutdown at United will mean for this town? We're talking about 3,000 jobs. There's no way that all of us can find work here. A lot of people will have to move away just to live.

LINDA: Three thousand! I hadn't realized it was that many. If what Hank says is true, we'll lose more than just a few members. *(Increasing concern in her voice)* With our building debt, the bank could foreclose on us!

PAUL: I don't mean to be callous here, but closing this church should be the least of our concerns! I understand Hank's concern for his family and their future because I'm concerned about my kids, too. Sally missed 15 days of school last year because of asthma attacks. She can't even breathe the air around here.

HANK: Paul, I'm sorry to hear about Sally's asthma. But you can move. You've got a college education. All I have is 20 years on a production line.

PAUL: It doesn't matter where I move. It doesn't matter if United has a plant there or not. Our lousy stewardship of this earth is making everybody sick. God has turned his back on us. And it can only get worse. If we don't draw the line there won't be any people — much less jobs.

LINDA: We're not getting anywhere here. The pastor came for some help. Let's take a break and try to cool down.

(A person steps out of the shadows and reads the following newspaper article to the audience.)

WORLD REPORT . . . "West Valley, the clean up continues."
West Valley, the site of one of the biggest illegal toxic dumps in the country is trying to recover from the effects of pollution. The Environmental Protection Agency said that all the barrels which had been stored at an abandoned factory have been removed but that the clean up is far from over. Leaks from the drums have seeped into the ground water and surrounding streams. Carcasses of fish and birds are still being recovered from the area. Residents have been advised to use bottled water until the level of contamination can be determined. In an interview last week, County Commissioner Smith said he was outraged at the health hazard the dump site is causing for area residents.

"I hope they catch whoever is responsible for this," said Smith. "West Valley used to be a great vacation spot for hunters and campers. Now it's not even safe to live here."

The EPA said that recovery from the environmental damage may take years. Meanwhile, area residents are asked to increase the number of physical examinations and to take extra precautions with children. Local health clinics are starting an information campaign on how to look for signs of contamination.

(The conversation at the table resumes.)

PASTOR: I don't know if we should cool down. We've been reacting with our hearts because we see just how much suffering can be caused by all of this. And as Christians, we know something about suffering because of Jesus. What would Jesus have us do beyond just being concerned?

LINDA: Well, if the plant shuts down we should certainly help the people with food and stuff.

HANK: Food alone won't do it, Linda. Even if all the churches worked together they couldn't provide for 3,000 unemployed families.

PAUL: We can provide pastoral counseling for the people in transition.

HANK: You're talking as if the only right thing to do was to shut the plant down.

PAUL: I'm sorry — but I think it would be best in the long run.

PASTOR: Hank, you know that the pollution can't go on — do you have something to offer?

HANK: Well, we've been talking about it at work. The company says it's too expensive to upgrade the pollution equipment. But if the community could pull together and provide the money to do that . . . .

PAUL: What about the mess that's already there? The town shouldn't have to bail out a company that has brought about its own destruction.

PASTOR: The company may have been irresponsible, but maybe they just lived by the then current standards which were too weak. We don't know if they were evil.

LINDA: And besides that Paul, you are the one who keeps saying that stewardship is the responsibility of everyone. We can't just point our collective religious finger of judgment. God calls us to do something. Somehow I think we have to help.

PASTOR: Maybe the churches could spearhead a movement to raise the money to upgrade the plant. There are thousands of Christians in town. We can all pitch in. Some are bankers like Paul, and there are lots of other business people. We can help them all see that this is a stewardship issue — that it does affect us all.

HANK: Thank you, Pastor. That's the most hopeful thing I've heard tonight. Do you really think we could do it?

PAUL: Maybe we could do it. But what happens in three years when the equipment is outdated again? We can't keep on bailing them out. It's just putting off the inevitable. They must be shut down.

LINDA: Maybe eventually they will have to shut down. At least this has us doing some positive things for people and the earth.

PASTOR: If nothing else, it buys us time to work on long range plans without destroying the community.

PAUL: Yeah. This would buy us time, but by then it may be too late.

HANK: If the plant closes, it's already too late.

PASTOR: It's not too late. It's never too late if we believe that God stands with us. We can't control this storm and it certainly won't go away. As a matter of fact, it will probably get worse before it gets better. But, God has promised to be with us. Let's begin to act like we believe it.

Section 2
Bible Study

Introduction

1 — Evangelism Bible Study

2 — Worship Bible Study

3 — Education Bible Study

4 — Social Concerns Bible Study

5 — Stewardship Bible Study

Introduction

In this chapter the resource explores discipleship through the study of five Bible passages from the Gospel of Mark. The studies pick up on the themes presented in the playlets, namely evangelism, worship, education, social outreach and stewardship. These Bible studies invite members of the congregation to explore their knowledge, feelings and sense of call towards the ministries of the church.

Each Bible study is primarily designed for small group study and has three segments.

Begin each study with prayer or other appropriate devotion.

Divide the class into groups of four to six people and assign one of the three study segments to each group.

Supply paper and pencils.

Allow for discussion and exploration within each group (15 minutes).

Call the entire class together and ask a member from each group to present group comments. Invite the whole class to add or clarify when the presenter is finished (10 minutes per group).

End the study by inviting the class to summarize. Have there been any surprises? Did they learn anything new? How do they feel about the particular ministry now? (10 minutes.)

Helpful hint: It may be advantageous to have the same study leader for all five sessions. However, the committee chairperson or someone involved in the ministry being discussed can be invited to help the study leader.

1 — Evangelism

Bible Study

Mark 1:4-8
John the Baptist appeared in the wilderness, preaching a baptism of repentance for the forgiveness of sins. And there went out to him all the country of Judea, and all the people of Jerusalem; and they were baptized by him in the river Jordan, confessing their sins. Now John was clothed with camel's hair, and had a leather girdle around his waist, and ate locusts and wild honey. And he preached, saying, "After me comes he who is mightier than I, the thong of whose sandals I am not worthy to stoop down and untie. I have baptized you with water; but he will baptize you with the Holy Spirit."

Focus your study on the witness to Christ, baptism and how we measure success.

1. Witness to Christ
a. John the Baptist pointed to Jesus. Has there been a John the Baptist in your life? How did he do it?
b. What are some of the ways you personally can point to Jesus?
c. John the Baptist was an outsider. He was dressed in strange clothes and ate strange things. Can you point to Christian witnesses who may not be taken seriously because they seem strange, i.e., fall outside of social norms?
d. Do you think that John had a special gift or skill that allowed him to witness to Jesus? Scripture says that not all are evangelists but that everyone who is baptized is a witness to Jesus. Make a list of how the baptized can witness to Jesus.

2. Baptism

a. John baptized with water for repentance and the forgiveness of sins. He said that Jesus would baptize with the Holy Spirit. What is the difference?

b. If you have been baptized in the name of Father, Son and Holy Spirit, what difference does it make to you as a person?

c. Is baptism really all that is needed to be a witness to Jesus? Why or why not?

3. Measuring Success

a. Many went out to hear John. Is this happening at your church? Why or why not?

b. Some say that faithful witness to Jesus cannot be "entertaining." Do you agree? Why or why not?

c. Have you ever been a John the Baptist (one who points to Jesus) for someone else? Tell your story. How did it make you feel?

d. What is the evangelism committee at your church doing to point to Jesus? What should the evangelism committee at your church be doing to point to Jesus?

e. How can you help?

2 — Worship

Bible Study

Mark 3:1-6
Again he entered the synagogue, and a man was there who had a withered hand. And they watched him, to see whether he would heal him on the Sabbath, so that they might accuse him. And he said to the man who had the withered hand, "Come here." And he said to them, "Is it lawful on the Sabbath to do good or to do harm, to save life or to kill?" But they were silent. And he looked around at them with anger, grieved at their hardness of heart, and said to the man, "Stretch out your hand." He stretched it out, and his hand was restored. The Pharisees went out, and immediately held counsel with the Herodians against him, how to destroy him.

Focus on the nature of worship, the worshipers, and some of the beliefs people hold about worship.

1. Worship as giving life

a. What is Jesus' basic complaint in the synagogue? Does he have a right to feel this way? Why?

b. Worship can be a healing and life-giving event. Are you healed or renewed at worship? How?

c. Do you think healing and renewal always happen? Why or why not?

d. What portions of the worship service are most healing or life-giving to you?

e. Sometimes worship may seem judgmental or simply so routine that we wish to turn away. How can renewal or healing come at such times? Or can it?

2. The Worshipers

a. Who needs healing? Many say that our hectic schedules are making us ill. Can our worship life address this? How?

b. Not everyone has a withered hand. What other kinds of infirmities do we bring to Jesus on Sunday morning? How do we ask for healing?

c. The man with the withered hand was also an outcast. Have you ever felt like an outcast at worship. Did anyone help you? How?

3. Beliefs about worship

a. Jesus did something that the religious people felt was unlawful on the Sabbath. What are some of the "laws" for worship? (Example: We all should come in our "Sunday best") Make a list.

b. Have you ever done something that other religious people considered "unlawful" or inappropriate on the Sabbath?

c. Why did you do it?

3 — Education

Bible Study

Mark 6:1-6

He went away from there and came to his own country; and his disciples followed him. And on the Sabbath he began to teach in the synagogue; and many who heard him were astonished, saying, "Where did this man get all this? What is the wisdom given to him? What mighty works are wrought by his hands! Is not this the carpenter, the son of Mary and brother of James and Joses and Judas and Simon, and are not his sisters here with us?" And they took offense at him. And Jesus said to them, "A prophet is not without honor, except in his own country, and among his own kin, and in his own house." And he could do no mighty work there, except that he laid his hands upon a few sick people and healed them. And he went about among the villages teaching.

Focus your attention on the teacher, the teachings and the audience or those who have come to hear.

1. Teachers

a. The people of Nazareth thought that Jesus did not have the proper credentials to be a teacher of the Word of God. We want good competent church school teachers for our programs. What kind of credentials or qualities should a church school teacher have? Make a list.

b. How do these qualities/credentials compare to Jesus?

c. How can the people of God help church school teachers do a good job?

d. Have you ever learned something from a person who was an unlikely teacher? Tell your story.

e. What do you remember best about your teachers at school and at church?

f. Jesus was rejected by his own people but he did not give up. The passage says that he went on teaching in the villages. Do you think church school teachers sometimes feel rejected? How? When? What do you think allows them to go on?

2. Teachings

a. At times Jesus' teachings themselves were rejected, even by the disciples. Tell a story of a time that you rejected a teaching of Jesus. (Example: Consider Matthew 5:22) Why did you reject it?

b. Give an example of a time that you smoothed over the rough edges of a teaching of Jesus because you were afraid of being rejected.

c. Do you think this happens in your church? How? When?

3. Audience/Hearers

a. How do the educational programs of your church tell Jesus' story? Is it always accepted? Why or why not?

b. What do you like about the educational programs of your church?

c. What don't you like about the educational programs of your church?

d. Make a list of some current social/world issues that you wish your church's educational programs would address. How could they do that in a Christian context?

4 — Social Concerns

Bible Study

Mark 12:28-34
And one of the scribes came up and heard them disputing with one another, and seeing that he answered them well, asked him, "Which commandment is the first of all?" Jesus answered, "The first is, 'Hear, O Israel: The Lord our God, the Lord is one; and you shall love the Lord your God with all your heart, and with all your soul, and with all your mind, and with all your strength.' The second is 'You shall love your neighbor as yourself.' There is no other commandment greater than these." And the scribe said to him, "You are right, Teacher; you have truly said that he is one, and there is no other but he; and to love him with all the heart, and with all the understanding, and with all the strength, and to love one's neighbor as oneself, is much more than all whole burnt offerings and sacrifices." And when Jesus saw that he answered wisely, he said to him, "You are not far from the kingdom of God." And after that no one dared to ask him any question.

Focus your study on the identity of the neighbor, the nature of your love for neighbor, and how your congregation as a whole cares for the neighbor.

1. Who are our neighbors?
a. Jesus tells us that those who love God and their neighbors as themselves are not far from the kingdom of God. Who are these neighbors that Jesus speaks about?
b. Who, in your opinion, are the neighbors who require our greatest attention?
c. Jesus seems to link love of God and love of neighbor. Do you make the same connection? Can you tell a story when you saw or experienced that connection?

2. Love of neighbor

a. Tell a story of when it was difficult to love or care for a neighbor. Why was it difficult?

b. How do you decide who deserves your love and compassion when only limited resources are available to you? Do you think Jesus would have done the same?

c. Tell a story of when you wished you could have done more for a neighbor. What prevented you from doing so?

d. Make a list of what expression your love of neighbor has taken. (Example: Giving money; visiting a sick person) What expression has given you the most satisfaction?

3. Your congregation's care of neighbor

a. Who are your church's neighbors?

b. How does your congregation put love of neighbor into action?

c. What do you think your church neglects to do for its neighbor?

d. How does your congregation decide whom to care for? Do you know all the projects your church's social concerns group is involved in? Make a list.

e. Is there anything you can do to help your church's social concerns group be faithful to Jesus' commandment?

5 — Stewardship

Bible Study

Mark 12:41-44
And he sat down opposite the treasury, and watched the multitude putting money into the treasury. Many rich people put in large sums. And a poor widow came, and put in two copper coins, which make a penny. And he called his disciples to him, and said to them, "Truly, I say to you, this poor widow has put in more than all those who are contributing to the treasury. For they all contributed out of their abundance; but she out of her poverty has put in everything she had, her whole living."

Focus on the widow's action, the nature of stewardship and how your congregation lives out the call to be stewards of God's gifts.

1. The widow's action
   a. The passage says that the widow gave away her entire livelihood. Do you think her action was good stewardship of her resources? How was she going to provide for herself?
   b. What could have been some of the widow's reasons for giving all she had? What are some of the reasons you give money to the church?
   c. How do you suppose other people make the decision to contribute to the church?
   d. Jesus says that all but the widow gave out of their abundance. Did he think the others did not give enough? That it wasn't the amount that counted but the sacrifice that was made? Or did he make no value judgment at all?

2. The nature of stewardship

a. There is more to stewardship than giving money. Give as many examples as you can.

b. The widow gave her whole livelihood. Are there ways other than money in which people give their whole livelihood to Jesus?

c. Tell a story in which you contributed something other than money to the church. Was it easier or more difficult than giving money? Explain.

d. What do you believe is your most precious resource?

3. Stewardship in your congregation

a. Does your congregation have an annual stewardship emphasis? What are some of the issues that come up?

b. If you were a member of the stewardship concerns group at your church, what issues would you like them to address? Why?

c. Is there a stewardship concern in your immediate community that you think your congregation should be involved in? (Example: Increase peoples' awareness about aluminum recycling; preserving park land)

d. Is there a stewardship concern in the world that you think your congregation should be involved in?

Section 3
Sermons

Introduction

Ash Wednesday — Come And See
     . . . The Day Of The Lord

Lent 1 — Come And See
     . . . The Wilderness

Lent 2 — Come And See
     . . . The King Who Weeps

Lent 3 — Come And See
     . . . The Way Of God

Lent 4 — Come And See
     . . . What The World Is Coming To

Lent 5 — Come And See
     . . . The Difference Of God

Introduction

The *Come And See* resource concludes with a series of six sermons, which move from Ash Wednesday through the five Sundays in Lent.

The sermons address some basic discipleship issues:

1. The tension between the necessities of daily life and the call to follow Jesus.

2. Focus on the Body of Christ as the place where disciples can find forgiveness, renewal, and are enabled to do God's work in the world.

3. The struggle to make sense of who this Jesus is that calls us.

The sermons for Sundays are based on gospel texts from the lectionary year "C." The sermon for Ash Wednesday uses the Old Testament as its basis.

Each sermon contains a brief summary at the beginning to help preachers find additional illustrations that are appropriate to their contexts.

Come And See
The Day Of The Lord

Ash Wednesday   **Joel 2:12-19**

(The prophet calls the community of God's people to repent and to live out the covenant.)

There is something about Ash Wednesday that makes this day different from any other day of the year. Even though for most of us Ash Wednesday began with schedules and busyness and work as usual, there is indeed one small sign that takes it out of the ordinary and routine. Today, in many churches, men, women, and children step forward to have a smudge of dark gray ashes placed on their foreheads. To be sure, a simple smudge of ashes is not much compared to the trumpet sound and the alarm of the prophet Joel which call the people of our first lesson to leave all that they are doing behind and to assemble for worship. "Blow the trumpet in Zion and gather all the people," the lesson says. "Let no one be excluded! Bring the leaders, the children, even the nursing infants and the bride and bridegroom from their honeymoon!"

Imagine it just for a moment. Imagine, if instead of just a smudge of ashes such a thing had happened in our town today. The sirens on top of the firehouse wailing and warning us to come to worship. Businesses and stores closing early so that everyone could make it to church; television and radio stations sounding the emergency broadcast signal instead of their usual programming; and teams of volunteers lining up to bring the aged, the infirm, and mothers with newborn infants.

But, of course, it didn't happen like that. Ash Wednesday began like any other workday in February and it is only a dark gray smudge of ashes on the foreheads of friends and neighbors that lets us know that something is different today.

Sometimes I would like to think that the very ordinariness of our Ash Wednesdays is a good sign; a sign which says that we are better off than the people whom the trumpet called together. The Old Testament tells us that they were a people of little hope. A plague of locusts had devoured their crops and stripped their fields so that only death prospered on their land. Their storehouses and cupboards and pots were bare, and the children went to bed hungry each night. There was not even sufficient grain to make an offering on the altar of God. And the people weren't even sure that it would make a difference anyway. It was as if God had forsaken his people. It was as if he had become their enemy. Is it any wonder then that the trumpet blew so urgently for one last summons: Let the people plead with God before disaster and destruction and failure overwhelms them all.

But, for us, there was no trumpet today! There was no firehouse siren or loud wailing. Only little dark smudges on our foreheads. Does that mean that we are better off — that our failures are smaller and our pain less severe? Does it mean that there is no hopelessness, no famine, no disaster, no forsakenness? Of course not — the ashes tell the story:

"I am an alcoholic who blew it again."

"My second divorce is inevitable."

"I have cancer."

"Again and again I fail at school."

"My kids went to bed hungry again last night."

"I got fired from my job."

"I can't forgive my brother."

"My mother should go to a nursing home but I promised I'd never do that to her."

"I'm always angry at the kids."

"I want to be perfect."

"I can't get rid of my guilt."

"I have AIDS."

We really aren't better off than the people in our lesson today. We still suffer. We still feel hopeless. We are in pain. And what makes our situation even worse than that of God's people in the Old Testament is that we don't allow the trumpet to sound or the siren to wail. We pretend that failures don't really exist as long as there is our ordinariness and schedules and busyness and routine. And we also hide the pain from one another — we turn our heads and close our ears lest someone else's imperfection reminds us uncomfortably of our own. Tonight, though, pain and failure and imperfection are difficult to ignore. They are a visible mark on the forehead of the one sitting next to you in the pew, on the co-worker at the office, on the stranger in the street. And these marks show us for who we are, a broken people whose insides are caught up in disaster and destruction and whose souls know of hunger and famine and forsakenness.

Today is Ash Wednesday and it came as any workday in February with schedules, and busyness and routine. But it is no ordinary day — for God has chosen to be with us.

"Rend your hearts, not your garments," God says. Rend your hearts — these words are not only full of the pain of tearing apart but also of tearing open, of offering who we are to the mercy of God. Rend your hearts and offer yourselves to the Lord for he is gracious and merciful, slow to anger, and abounding in steadfast love. And it isn't just to him that such an offering can be made. It is also to one another, for who can better understand what lives under that smudge than one who bears the same sign. God has called us into fellowship under the smudge of ashes — the sign of brokenness. He has called us to be with one another, to fill the empty places in the soul, to heal the pain and forgive the failures. He has called us to visit the woman with cancer and to bring her a measure of hope. He asks us to speak to the brother whose life is full of shame and guilt and tell him that his sins are forgiven. He wants us to support and comfort the one who lost a job. And he wishes us to feed the hungry and touch the body dying of AIDS. And if we do so then the fellowship of brokenness will know not only pain, but also the mercy and graciousness of God, and also his steadfast love.

Today is Ash Wednesday and our journey into Lent begins. It is the journey that will take Jesus to Jerusalem and death. And if we are willing to follow him we just might see that it is no accident that the dark grey smudge on the forehead is in the shape of a cross. The smudge, the sign of brokenness, the mark of fellowship, is also a sign of solidarity with the Jesus who was God but who chose to share in everything we are, including our failures and our frustration and our pain.

Today is Ash Wednesday, and it came as any workday in February with busyness and schedules and routine. It did not come with trumpet calls or wailing sirens or emergency broadcast signals. But I wish it had. I wish it not because I want to summon everyone to plead one more time with God. But I wish it because then everyone could have heard God's word of mercy and grace and steadfast love. Ultimately that word is what makes Ash Wednesday no ordinary day at all. That word makes it the day of the Lord. Amen.

Come And See The Wilderness

First Sunday In Lent   Luke 4:1-13

(God's spirit drives Jesus into the wilderness and temptation. The temptations show Jesus' humanness and complete identification with our life situation.)

Can you believe it? Already it is the first Sunday in Lent! I have hardly had time to enjoy my Christmas presents, much less pay for them, and already it is Lent. The solemn services of Ash Wednesday certainly got my attention and reminded me of my origins in dust. But sometimes the church seasons and traditions seem to run together like a lot of trivia in a very active life that challenges me to survive and remain sane.

Indulge me along that line of thinking for just a moment. Pretend that we are playing "Trivial Pursuit" and you need a game piece for religion. At the junior level, almost any American could recount the Christmas story with some detail. At the regular adult level, most of us could probably combine the various details of the Easter story and get it right. On a master level we could answer questions about the color of the paraments for the various church seasons or even the particular Scripture lessons that are suggested for specific Sundays. If this is the first Sunday in Lent, then our "Trivial Pursuit" answer is that we read about the temptations of Jesus.

But the temptations of Jesus aren't a trivial matter and neither is the pursuit of the story's meaning for us. Today, from Luke, we remember the confrontation between Satan and Jesus after 40 days alone in the wilderness. There is the simple invitation for Jesus to take care of himself.

"Change some stones into bread. Relieve your hunger."

Or, speaking of power, Satan offers the power to rule over all the earth in exchange for the acknowledgement of Satan's own power.

Then, too, there is the innocent urging to boldly trust God — or is it to test God? Jesus could and should throw himself down so that the angels who have charge over him can fulfill God's promise and save Jesus from death.

We remember this story because of Sunday school teachers, parents and preachers. And we remember this story because we are so familiar with temptation ourselves. Unlike the miracle stories of feeding, healing and forgiving which are so wonderful but also so far away, temptation is at my right hand all the time.

The children start arguing five minutes after I'm in the door from a difficult day at work. I am tempted to simply yell at them to be quiet. Or I am tempted to ignore the verbal abuse they sling at each other as I move for the newspaper and my favorite chair in the living room. All of the time I feel that what I ought to do is sit down with the children, invite them to tell their stories, and try with the wisdom of Solomon to separate fact from fiction and turn the fighting into better feelings. Ha! My life is littered with trials and temptations and failures.

Since my early teens I have been fighting a compulsion to overeat and to be overweight. Just when I think that I have my life plan for food going in the right direction, a co-worker arrives with a birthday cake or Sunday school children bake Valentine's cookies and beg me to take just one. My special weakness is chocolate and without fail this temptation comes with each trip to the grocery store. Just when I think that I have done a good job and that I am home free, it happens. The person in front of me stops to write a check or questions the price of the laundry detergent. Meanwhile, another shopper has pulled in behind me and there I am — stuck between grocery carts, the conveyor belt and the candy display with its 16 varieties of chocolate bars.

Maybe Jesus could withstand the temptation, but I can't. He was the Son of God, I am only human. And then six candy bars go on the conveyor and with the motor starts the downward spiral of added calories, added guilt and added weight.

That is the kind of reasoning many of us do when confronted with temptation. That is the kind of thinking that makes it all a trivial pursuit. Luke's story about Jesus' temptation is filled with power and good news. Power and news that are in no way trivial.

First of all, Luke tells us that an agent of God is involved here. The same Spirit of God that descends and brings Jesus a blessing at his baptism is the Spirit that drives Jesus into the wilderness. This is no mistake for Jesus. This is not a random event like me getting caught in the grocery story. This is the purposeful act of God through the Spirit. For what? This is to perfect that which God is doing in Jesus. Clearly the Son of God had the power to change stones to bread. Surely he could exercise that power and authority to rule the earth. Certainly he could choose to separate himself from his father and have spiritul authority of his own.

God was risking everything in this test of Jesus, this turning point for Jesus . . . and for all humanity. No, this is not a silly little story about being tempted to cheat on a diet or tell a little white lie. Here the very hope of God to save his creation through an obedient son is on the line at this point and it is the Spirit who drives Jesus to this point.

Do you get the point for us? Baptized, secured by God and empowered by the Holy Spirit, Jesus is immediately (but not once and for all) put to the test. Not just any old test like a math exam or a drug test whose results will place you in algebra or the unemployment line, but the test of all history which will seal not only Jesus' fate but all humanity's. And it is the Spirit that drives Jesus into the wilderness, into the test site. You know the story. Jesus passes with flying colors.

Is the point that Jesus is the model of the godly life, the example of what God expects of us? Demands of us? If that is true, if that is where the story stops then we say hurray for him, but woe to me and you. For we plainly know how often we have and do fail the tests of faith when driven to the wilderness areas of our own lives. Whether we are aware of it or not, the Spirit constantly drives us to our limits to test us, strengthen us, perfect us in our own faith as God brings his future into our present moment. In that way Jesus shares with us everything we are. Know this, the testing will always be around things that happen in our own wilderness of life — things that are important for survival, things that we consider the necessities of life — food, or self interest, power, or self position in the community, and spirituality — going life alone or with God and his community.

The Spirit drives us out to the wilderness when the boss tells us to work another 65-hour week. We must choose. Will we abandon family and faith to keep the job going and the paycheck coming, or will we trust God for this necessity of life? When the Spirit drives you to the edge where you are offered a promotion at work or a special assignment at school, will you take it at the price of putting down or running over a co-worker or fellow student? Or can you put aside the promotion and the prestige to live the servant life rather than that of the slave master? And in your faith, when the Spirit drives you to the edge, as you begin to wonder if you really need to be in the Bible study or even at worship Sunday mornings, couldn't you do just as well at home in prayer and Bible reading?

Luke's account of Jesus' temptation helps us set the stage for all of our Lenten reflection. Temptation is a universal part of life from the trivia of a chocolate bar to the throbbing, nagging questions of doubt and hopelessness. We must never underestimate the power of sin and evil. More importantly, we must never underestimate the power and love of God for all the baptized children everywhere. As surely as the Spirit is sent to drive us to the tests and trials of life, the failure of any of the tests, trials or suffering of this world can be confessed to and redeemed by the one who died so that we might live fully and eternally. Whatever the test, no matter how miserable the failure, nothing can separate us from the love of God which is in Christ Jesus our Lord.

Jesus' victory in today's story does not provide a measuring stick for our judgment and despair as we fail, pass and fail.

His obedience reminds us of the Spirit's testing and God's unwillingness to give in to evil.

It's the first Sunday in Lent. We've heard again about the temptation of Jesus . . . and his growing power to love and save us in our sin. Can you believe it? This is no trivial pursuit. Amen.

Come And See
The King Who Weeps

Second Sunday In Lent   Luke 13:31-35

(Even as Jesus' life is threatened, he continues to help and to heal. He laments the stubbornness of people in every generation who reject the power of God's love.)

Don was his father's delight. Marge and Fred had hopes and prayed for a happy, healthy baby and their prayers were answered. Don cooed and smiled and giggled. He was attentive. He was pleasant. He was everything that any parents would hope for in their firstborn; in any child for that matter.

As Don grew there was a special bonding between him and his dad. It may have started with the first hug and words in the delivery room but it also grew each day. Every moment Don was a joy to Fred. It was fun to feed Don. It was fun to watch him struggle to grasp new objects as well as concepts like, "good boy!" Fred and Don wrestled on the floor and out in the yard. They played catch after they had helped wash and dry the dinner dishes.

Fred's heart ached the first day that Don went off to kindergarten but he put on a strong face, a happy smile and lots of encouragement for his son whom he loved. But school was tough on Don. He didn't know how to settle a dispute and often had to run to the teacher for help — help freely given. Here and around the neighborhood he began to see that life is not always safe or true or just. He learned, too, the importance of parental power.

One of the bigger kids at the bus stop made fun of Don's small size. When he saw that Don was uncomfortable with that kind of attention, he played all the harder. He took Don's homework one day. Don got a bad grade, a knot in his stomach and one tear down the side of his face. A tear that Fred didn't notice when he questioned his son about the assignment. Finally, after the bully had taken his lunch and his homework one too many times, Don told his father what had been happening.

That night, Don saw a new and wonderful side of his dad. After dinner, instead of playing catch, Fred and Don walked up to the bully's house. Don almost shook with terror when the bully answered the door. But the tables turned quickly and Don stood tall at his father's side.

"Young man," Fred said, "I want to speak with you and your father."

The bully started to fidget, got an inspiration, and said, "He's not home right now."

The words were hardly out of his mouth when George, the boy's dad, came up from the basement saying, "Who's at the front door?"

Don watched his father, the bully and his dad as Fred got right to the point. "George, your son is a bully and a liar. He terrorizes Don at the bus stop each day. He has ripped Don's homework for the fun of it, taken his lunch repeatedly and just now said you weren't home when I asked to talk to you. I know that you will do the right thing and that we won't have to talk about trouble between these kids again."

George was speechless. Without a word he turned and smacked his son hard, on the face. Tears came quickly. George started to swing again but Fred grabbed the other man's arm in midair and said calmly but firmly, "I'm sure that you and your son have a lot to talk about."

Fred put his arm around Don's shoulder, turned and left their neighbor's house. They didn't need to say a word. Don had just seen his father "blow the bully away." But adults can always do that to kids. That's what George was about to do to his own son when Fred had exercised his power against another adult! "Wow," Don thought, "my dad has got to be the best, the meanest, the toughest father in the world!"

That night, just before he fell off to sleep, Don thought about the day and the days of pain and terror before. He was glad that his father was strong, powerful, decisive. He was glad that his father knew what to say and do. That he knew about injustice and how to treat it among kids and adults. He was glad . . . as he drifted into sleep.

If early childhood was idyllic, the teenage years and young adulthood were disastrous as far as many friends, neighbors and school officials were concerned. No one was quite sure where it started or even when or how, but Don was different. Fred knew it and so did everyone else. Don always needed to push the rules to their limits. When he had a curfew he would show up a few minutes late, then later and later. He hung out with a rough crowd. He was accused of cheating on his final exams in high school. When he came back from his first few weeks at college, Don looked terrible. Fred couldn't believe his eyes. Don was unshaven, his clothes were dirty, his hair was long over his shoulders and he brought a girl with him for the weekend. She looked and smelled worse than Don did.

Fred spoke firmly and clearly to his son, "Your mother and I have missed you. Come in, get cleaned up and let's talk about what you've been doing at school."

"Nothing much to talk about. School is a real party. Star, here, and I were bored so we thought we'd come over here for some good food and TV," Don said as he brushed past his father and into the kitchen for the refrigerator.

That weekend was bad but the times got even worse. Don wrecked his car going back to school after a party. His grades just barely kept him from academic probation. Rumors were everywhere that Don was a bad apple. He was doing drugs and dealing. Star was pregnant. Fred and his wife were heart-broken. Especially Fred.

One might, Marge and Fred were on the way to a dinner party up the street at George's. "I remember the time Don and I came up here to confront George about his son's behavior. Life was so simple then. Kids were good or bad. You told them the right things to do and to be. They listened," Fred mused to Marge and the silence of his own soul.

George must have been thinking about that, too. After light conversation by the wet bar, George handed Fred his drink and said, "It seems like just yesterday you gave me some real good advice about my kid — being a bully and all. Time really flies." George paused but pushed on, a man with a mission, a man with a cause, a man with real insight. "You know, Fred, you could probably use some good advice about that boy of yours right about now. Don't you think it's about time you tell him to shape up or ship out? I mean, everybody is saying that he is dealing drugs and that he got that girl pregnant. You know he's just trouble. If he were my son I'd beat some sense into him or at least I'd made darn sure that he didn't come home until he got his act together." George's voice was louder than he realized. His wife and Marge had stopped their conversation and stood breathlessly, not knowing what to expect.

Fred put his glass down. He looked George right in the eye — not to challenge him to a fight but to engage him into a wholly different world. He said, "George, if Don were your son, I might just do that. But he is my son and I will wait." A tear ran silently over his cheek as all four of them stood in silent pain.

Today, on the second Sunday of Lent, we see again the power and the pain of a father's love for his children. Young or old, it is comforting to know the power of God and to experience him coming as a king with justice in his hands. God's throne of judgment and his might through eternity make the evil ones tremble and the innocent victims rejoice with hope for justice.

But when we are caught in sin, torn up by fear, doubt or pain, there can be nothing more comforting than the sight not of the king but of his saving son weeping over a belligerent and rebellious people whom his father had called again and again through prophets and priests.

Indeed we need a Lord to rule the world and our hearts with kingly might. But even more, we need a savior and friend who will call to us even with tears of pain and death in his eyes. Such a savior we have in Christ Jesus. Amen.

Come And See The Way Of God

Third Sunday In Lent
Luke 13:1-9
Exodus 3:1-8b, 10-15

(God's way of running the kingdom is certainly different from how we run the world.)

A couple of weeks before Christmas I took an hour off from work one afternoon to run a few errands for my family. As I was walking through the parking lot of the shopping center I heard this booming voice behind me:

"My God, you're a woman priest!" I turned around and there, standing about 10 feet away from me was a young man who looked as if he had just seen an apparition.

"You're a woman priest! I've never seen a woman priest before!" he shouted again over the tops of several cars.

I really didn't know what to say to him. Finally I just blurted out:

"Yes, and it is Christmas, too."

"That it is!" he yelled back. "Merry Christmas to you!"

I guess I really got this young man's attention with my strange attire. And this wasn't the first time that someone had been stopped in their tracks for a moment to see a woman in an outfit that had been worn exclusively by men for almost 2,000 years. One time, to my utter embarrassment, my attire reduced a young Roman Catholic cashier at a fast food restaurant to speechlessness. And people always ask me what my title is:

"Do I call you Father or Mother or Sister or what?"

As I ran my errands that day I thought again about how the clerical clothes I wear are a very public and visible sign, not just to the church, but to all people, that things are changing, that the church is becoming more inclusive, that it is trying hard to tell the world that women are equal partners in the ministry of this Body of Christ.

Today's Scripture lessons, too, are about witness and attention getting; like my clerical clothes they are about grabbing someone, arresting them in their path, making them draw in their breath for a moment and taking notice. Only it is not me or us who do the grabbing, it is God who has something to say and needs us to pay attention.

In our Old Testament lesson for example there is the spectacular attention grabber of the burning bush — a bush that is alight with fire but not consumed, bright, but not hot, aflame, but not burned. The whole spectacle is designed by God to get Moses away from tending the sheep and turning him towards God and the future of the people of Israel. In our Epistle lesson Paul is telling the Corinthian church of the magnanimous deeds of God — how God had let manna rain from heaven in the wilderness, and how water had poured forth from the rocks in the desert, and how the miraculous bronze serpent healed those who were sick. Even the parable that Jesus tells to the people surrounding him is about attention getting and attention giving — the attention that the gardener is giving to the fig tree though it has yet to bear fruit.

This whole list of fantastic deeds and fanfare that, particularly, our epistle lesson recounts today made me wonder about whether one of God's main frustrations with his people, with us, is our unwillingness or inability or plain denseness when it comes to listening or paying attention to him. Does God have to resort to grandiose displays because there is no other way to arrest us in our tracks? The Bible is full of stories of God calling us with little success, stories about wooing us with love and when that did not work, of sending us outrageous fireworks, and when that did not do it of sending us loud and eccentric prophets, and when that failed of finally coming himself and marching us up to a hill to witness his own execution to make the point:

"Look, it is I, God. I love you and need you. Can't you see that?"

I have to admit that as a preacher of the gospel I know a little bit of that frustration, too. There have been times when after 15 or 20 counseling appointments I have realized that I might as well have been talking to the couch because the person who sits across from me is in such trouble that I cannot help them at all. There have been times when I preached at least 30 sermons on God's faithfulness and care and concern and I visit someone in the hospital who has heard most of these sermons but says that God is punishing him with illness because of past misdeeds and sins.

I think I am not the only one who knows about such frustration. If you are a parent like I am, you know how difficult it can be sometimes to get your child's attention. You ask the child 20 times not to bounce the ball in the house only to find that your youngster is doing it again, and so you can't stand it anymore and you grab him and look him straight in the eye and say: "I told you not to do that anymore!"

Those are the times when your insides are all churning and you wish you had some magic to make the child stop and listen so that the message would stick. All of us know God's frustration! All of us have had experiences where it seemed that no matter what we said or did — stand on our heads, repeat ourselves until the mouth is dry, dance a jig, stomp our feet, shout and wave our arms — there was no effect. And those are the times when we have wished that we would have that burning bush at our disposal, something so bright and spectacular that, like Moses, no one could turn away and disregard it.

However, we don't have a burning bush at our disposal; and besides that, the message of today's texts would be pretty awful if the story ended there, if all we heard as a message today was that we are as barren as the fig tree when it comes to listening to God. You see, despite the fact that God sends signs and things still go wrong, despite the fact that neither the burning bush, nor the manna, nor the prophets, nor even the cross ever seem a lasting sign, God keeps on trying no matter what. Each Lent he calls us out of our complacency, away from the notion that his work or ours is done as long as we have brothers and sisters who suffer from oppression and injustice and hunger. Each Sunday he calls before us the gospel, the Word that says:

"No, this disease is not a punishment for your sins. As a matter of fact, I will be with you through this. I will shoulder your burden, I will walk with you through your doubt and uncertainty and pain and hopelessness."

That is the point of the texts.

And each time he meets us at the communion table and in the waters of baptism he lets us know that he is willing to die to meet us there. That's the point of the story.

In the parable that Jesus tells today, what emerges loud and clear is not so much the frustration over the barrenness of the tree, but the gardener's, and therefore God's, willingness to try one more time, to be patient and nourish the tree for another year, to try again and again. And in our epistle lesson also, Paul reminds his brothers and sisters that God is faithful, that he will not abandon those he calls his own. And finally, in the story of Moses, God tells him that he will not let Moses go to Pharaoh alone. The bush isn't a once-and-for-all-time message. No, God will go with Moses and the people as they begin their journey out of Egypt.

"I am who I am," God says. It is his name, his title. It is the name of him who is not just the God of the ancestors, of the past, but also the God of the future, the God who will bring the Israelites out of Egypt and into freedom. For God there is no story of frustration and failed attempts, but the proclamation of who he is: the story of him who keeps on calling and flaunting his stuff and blowing the trumpet until we turn around and stop what we are doing and listen and look.

It might very well be that God does not send burning bushes too often, at least not anymore, but he does send women in black clerics to tell the world that we are all equal and precious in his sight. And he does send men and women who have arms to carry food, and give hugs, mouths to proclaim his faithfulness and extend welcomes and who have hearts full of courage so that his justice is told and his will is done.

I guess ultimately the most spectacular display, the brightest burning bush that ought to get our attention today is the fact that God doesn't get tired of it all, that he doesn't give up, that he will not be satisfied unless he has tried one more time, one more Sunday, one more Lent, one more year. Amen.

Come And See
What The World Is Coming To

Fourth Sunday In Lent　　　Luke 15:1-3, 11-32

(Some of Jesus' contemporaries said that he moved among the wrong kind of people. In the familiar story of a father and two sons, we hear again how life is changed by sin and kingdom love.)

When I walked into the kitchen at church to get another bowl of soup at our mid-week Lenten soup supper I saw Hank on his knees pushing at the dishwashing machine and Wayne with a rag mop ready to swab the deck of the good ship St. John's church. Both men were still dressed from the day's work, at the office for Hank and on the road, selling, for Wayne. Suit coats were off. Shirt sleeves were rolled up. Ties were now loose around their necks. I thought I had walked into the church kitchen. It was more like a hornet's nest.

"I didn't know that you guys worked on the property committee," I said with a breeze of humor. Sharp glances and thinly veneered anger flashed back from Hank.

"No, pastor, we're not on the property committee, but somebody had to fix this mess," he said.

Wayne joined in, "Every year you want to have these things and every year something goes wrong that Hank and I have to fix."

"These things?" I queried innocently.

"These Lenten suppers," Hank said. "I'm sure it's a great idea on paper, pastor, but there are always problems. Sometimes there's not enough soup. Sometimes strangers come and don't know how the system works. Always there is a mess in the kitchen."

Wayne chimed in, "It's as if everyone likes to party but nobody likes to take the time or makes the effort to plan these things or to help out when things go badly. If it weren't for Hank and me tonight, the place would probably be under a couple of inches of water right now. The dishwashing machine backed up and made this terrible mess, but everyone just went along their merry way as if nothing had happened. Listen to them out there! They're just laughing and eating and having a great time while we're in here slopping around in dirty dish water."

"Do you want me to try to find you some help?" I asked.

"No," Hank said from his prayer-like position in front of the dishwasher. "I've just about got it now. But it does make you wonder what this world is coming to."

"Yeah," Wayne added emphatically. "I think that everyone took you seriously on Sunday with that sermon about the ring, the robe and the sandals. Folks are acting like royalty rather than partners in this church family. Every year more and more people come to these things but fewer and fewer people help in the kitchen. Madge said that she is fed up! She's not making soup next year."

Concerned for these men and their strong feelings and intrigued by the connection with my sermon, I asked, "What did you hear me say on Sunday, Wayne?"

Hank answered. "The same thing that you and every preacher before you has said: that it's okay to go out and squander your life and your time and all of your resources because God is going to forgive you just like the father forgave and welcomed the young son in the parable that Jesus told."

Defensively I said, "Hank, that's not what I said and you know it. That sounds like an open invitation for people to go out and do whatever they want to do."

"It might not be what you meant to say, but that's what I heard," Hank continued.

"And you say it in lots of ways," added Wayne. "There are many of us who were here long before you came and, God willing, will be here long after you move on to a bigger church. The prodigal gets all of the good press and folks like us never get anything."

I realized that these guys were serious about their faith and about their pain as well as the dishwasher repair. I tried to think of ways to at least get them out of the kitchen and into the fellowship of the next room so that they wouldn't feel so put upon. Before I could say a word, Hank sang a new verse of the same song.

"You know why this dishwasher backed up, pastor? It's because those people from the baby shower didn't read the instructions. They didn't clean out the filter screen after their party. Now I'm up to my ankles in dirty dish water."

"Speaking of that shower, Sally was shocked," Wayne offered. "Here some 17-year-old girl gets pregnant and somebody in the church thinks she needs a party. I tell you, there wouldn't have been a party if that were my daughter. We would have at least kept the pregnancy quiet. But nooo! Instead of hushing up this sex scandal, somebody decides to have a party. And have it at church of all places!"

"And clogs up this dishwasher." Hank interjected.

"What's this world coming to, anyway?" Wayne said to no one in particular.

"That somebody was me," I said.

"What are you talking about, pastor?" Wayne asked.

"I'm the one who asked some of the folks in the congregation to have a baby shower for Cheryl," I said.

"There," said Hank, "I've got this thing fixed and you've just made my point."

"I wasn't trying to make your point, Hank," I protested. "Let me try to help you see why I did what I did for Cheryl. She's just a kid."

"My point exactly," grinned Hank.

"A kid who made a wrong decision," I went on. "She let her hormones lead the way instead of her head. Her family never has shown much love or concern for her. Now they have thrown her out emotionally and physically. I thought some people at church could help her find a place to live, get some things for the baby and most importantly, show her some real love."

Wayne started to soften. "Okay, pastor, we all make mistakes. And I guess I'm glad that folks from church are going to help her. But did we have to make such a big deal of it? You could have just asked around. Even I would have kicked in a hundred bucks on the sly."

"But she needs more than money," I protested.

"You've got that part right, pastor. She needs a good talking to about sex and morality and responsibility," Hank said. "Not a party where they make her think it's okay to do that. A party where they don't even take care of the church property."

Wayne came back into the conversation. "What's the world coming to, pastor? Hank and I and lots of other folks here at church work real hard every day. We try to make a decent living to support our families. We try to lead good lives. But we are always taken for granted. Not that you have to make a big deal over us, but you seem to be more interested in the newcomers and all of the weirdos that come around here than you are with those of us who have put our hearts and souls into this place most of our lives."

"Just like the parable on Sunday, pastor," Hank added.

"You guys are sounding like the elder brother in the story." I said.

"Pastor, that's the way we feel," said Wayne. "And I don't hear any good news in that story for us or the other people like us. What's the point of working hard, leading a decent life and then getting told it doesn't matter?"

"Wait a minute, Wayne," I protested sharply. "Jesus never said that it didn't matter and I hope that I didn't say that either. What he showed us in the elder brother was the fact that he was just as far away from home as his kid brother who had actually gone into a far away country."

"I'm not following you, pastor," Wayne said as he pushed the mop over the last little puddle of water on the floor.

"Then you weren't following Sunday, either, Wayne," Hank joined in. "Even I got that much from the sermon. The elder boy's jealousy and anger kept him from being close to his father or his brother. He made himself a self-imposed foreigner. He chose not to be with his father and brother just like the young kid — just for different reasons."

"That's right," I said. "And he even talked about how he had slaved over the farm while the young boy was away. The older son took himself too seriously. So seriously that he didn't act like a son or a brother. He acted . . ."

"Like a fool," Hank finished the sentence with his words.

"That's a pretty harsh judgment, Hank. I would have said he acted poorly, or childishly or immaturely. I don't think that I would have said, 'fool'," I responded.

"Why not?" asked Wayne. "Are you too much of a politician for that kind of straight talk?"

"No, Wayne," I answered. "This is too close to home for me. The elder brother didn't die 2,000 years ago as far as I am concerned. Part of that personality or style or whatever is still a big part of who I am and how I act. Sometimes I get so wrapped up in my church work that I get to thinking that no one else can do it or that no one else cares as deeply as I do. I get pretty frustrated when I think about all of the talented people here at our church who don't do much for the Lord except worship a few times each year. I get angry and jealous and sad to think about all of the families that go to Florida and have nice homes and nice cars and nice clothes but who would never seriously think about the joy of giving 10 percent of their income to the Lord's work. Then I get embarrassed about my feelings because they make me sound so petty and self-righteous."

The three of us got real quiet in a strange and awkward way there in the church kitchen with wet mops, rolled-up sleeves and newly-bared souls.

Then Hank spoke. Maybe he was trying to care for me. Maybe he was just trying to get out of the awkwardness. Who knows? Maybe he was just trying to justify his own lifestyle, but I don't think so.

"Pastor, that's nothing to be embarrassed about. That's exactly what Wayne and I have been saying. If you didn't worry and work the way that you do and if we didn't dig in and fix and fuss the way that we do, the whole place would probably fall apart and you know it."

"Maybe," I said. "But Jesus says trust him. Live like a son or a daughter, not like a slave. We don't have to justify ourselves or our work before God or anyone else. He gives us all that we are, all that we need and more! We can live with him in peace and joy rather than with all of this fear of failure and self examination."

"Yeah, but he gives the young kid a party. It's not fair!" Wayne protested.

"You're right, Wayne," I said. "It's not fair. It's more than fair. It's reckless. It's extravagant. It's wonderful. And just like the father went out and invited the young son in before he could say his rehearsed piece, the father went out to the elder son, too, and invited him to come in. When the kingdom of God comes near, everyone is invited in for the celebration and it's not complete until everyone is there. As a matter of fact, why don't we go in and have some dessert and enjoy this celebration?"

When the three of us came out of the kitchen together and smiling, some folks didn't know what to say. I guess they expected a hornet's nest. Then, I saw one long-time member look up at us and I heard her whisper to her neighbor, "Look at that. What's this world coming to, anyway?" Amen.

Come And See The Difference Of God

Fifth Sunday In Lent   Luke 20:9-19

(Jesus tells us a story about his own death — a death which is the faithful climax of God's faithful dealings with a violent and sinful world.)

I had a friend in seminary who is a much better biblical scholar than I am. I used to ask him where to locate a particular saying or story that I could recite from memory but could not find in my Bible. And my friend Joe was also very fond of odd bits and pieces of information — in our circle of friends he was defintely the undisputed champ at "Trivial Pursuit." One of the odd bits of information that Joe liked to collect was what he called "the most offensive text in the Bible."

I think that Joe asked every one of my seminary professors that question, and probably everyone else at the seminary as well. At last count he had quite a collection of texts. Well, today, I would like to put in my vote for a text that offends and scares me and which causes me trouble in understanding and preaching. Today's parable of the wicked tenants defintely gets my vote as belonging in Joe's category — except that this is not a fun game or to be taken lightly.

One of my seminary professors once said during class that Jesus was killed for telling stories. We all thought that the professor was having an off-day when he made the remark, but it was sure ringing in my ears when I started to work with this text for a sermon. It actually did not begin that way: both the Old Testament lesson and Paul's message to the Philippians sound not only hopeful, but downright jubilant. In the Old Testament, the prophet addresses a down-trodden, exiled people, telling them that God is working right this very minute to release them from their captors, to give them a new exodus and a return to the promised land. And in Philippians Paul talks about the surpassing worth of knowing Jesus Christ as Lord:

"I was the best Pharisee, the best lawyer, the best scholar, the best at everything," says Paul. "But I count it all as refuse, trash, when compared to knowing and finding Christ, and living in relationship with him."

Again there is this sense of exuberance and jubilation. And then I came to the gospel lesson and my professor's remark about Jesus being killed for telling stories started to ring in my ears. What goes on in this story, and why in the world was it placed together with those two other texts? Granted, there is a kind of escalation, a kind of "You ain't seen nothing yet" in all three texts, but in the gospel it is not a hopeful or exuberant affair. It is not a new exodus for an exiled people, not Paul celebrating his growing relationship with his Lord. Here we have an escalation of violence and brutality and abuse, an escalation that starts with a beating and ends with murder.

Three times the owner of the vineyard sends servants to the tenants to collect the rent, but one after another is beaten up and wounded and sent away empty-handed. Three times — and that is only half of the story, a story which does not seem to make much sense.

On the one hand there is the open callousness and brutality of the tenants. There are no excuses, the "check-is-in-the-mail" kind of talk. Quite the contrary, it seems that these people have no fear of authority, no fear that someone will come and take them to court and jail so that justice will be served. And on the other hand there is the seemingly outright foolishness of the landowner. Why didn't he call the authorities after his first servant was beaten up? Why did he expose a second and third person to the same danger? Why didn't the owner use a force equal to that of the tenants? That is what we would have done! We would have seen to it that the violence did not harm our household any further.

Unfortunately, that is not how Jesus tells this story. As a matter of fact, the owner does what you or I would never have done. The owner sends the child, his own son, his heir, in the hopes that the tenants will respect him and turn over the rent money. And what happens? The tenants murder the son. Their greed has no limits and they murder the son!

Why would Jesus tell such a crazy story? And what is it all about? Does the story want to tell us that the landowner is God and that we are the wicked tenants who have no regard for justice, who are greedy and brutal and show no mercy? Are we the ones who cannot tell right from wrong? Some of Jesus' audience thought that the story was about them. The last verse in today's text says that the scribes and chief priests wanted to arrest Jesus as soon as the story came out of his mouth. Jesus was killed for telling stories, my professor once said in class.

But Jesus could not possibly have spoken to us. We do have respect for the law. We rely on the proper authorities, we don't take what does not belong to us. We pay our bills and at worst we might be guilty of an occasional "The check-is-in-the-mail" kind of talk. We are not a violent and brutal people. Jesus could not possibly have meant us! But what if he did? What if it is not outright violence and brutality that makes us the tenants of the story but our tolerance of all such things — like when we are silent accomplices when the violence and inhumanity happens somewhere else; when our environment is destroyed and we keep silent because we just don't want to do without this convenience or that gadget; or when we allow powerful nations to deplete the resources of poorer, helpless ones and we don't speak up because our standard of living might be affected; or when we are careful to keep out own neighborhoods relatively free of crime and abjection and don't do anything when the violence happens somewhere else. Our faith demands that we speak up, our baptism asks us to participate in the process of bringing about greater justice and equality and yet often we shut our eyes and mouths and keep idle. What if Jesus meant us? What if we don't give what is due to God? What if that is the way we refuse to pay the rent?

Then the story does sound offensive — offensive enough that pastors and preachers think twice about making the connection between us and the tenants of the story. Such connections have been capable of causing dissension in our churches:

"I don't come to church to hear such stuff. I don't need to be accused like that. What right does the pastor have to tell me that I am an accomplice to violence and injustice? I've never laid a hand on anybody."

It is offensive and can't we all hear the outrage of the scribes and chief priests in our own language?

But we must not stop here. The outrage of the scribes might be ours too but we will not reach the same conclusion. For as Jesus tells it, the story of the vineyard, or his own story as the Son of God is not merely an accusation of how we fail God, but also a story of how God does not fail us. Even after the servants have been wounded and cast out, God does not invoke legal sanctions. He does not retaliate in kind. He does not answer violence with violence. Instead he sends the Son. God faithfully continues the relationship he has established with us even if it means to take repeated beatings, even if it means that in the end he will have to sacrifice the child. God does not waver from what he has set out to do. God does not only love the righteous ones and the good ones, but God even loves his enemies: those who tell him that the check is in the mail, the liars, the cheaters, the thieves, the silent accomplices, and yes, even the murderers. He is the God of the cross, not the God of glory. And that truly is the ultimate offense of the parable because it has nothing to do with justice but only with grace.

In the end this parable ought to leave us both with a warning and a hope. The warning is that as far as God is concerned our struggles to hang on to all those little vineyards, the conveniences, the gadgets, the lifestyles and successes won't mean anything in the kingdom. They are just games, odd bits of information, trivial pursuit or as Paul says in the epistle, trash, refuse, worthless. They won't be tolerated in the kingdom. The parable says so.

But at the same time, God's grace and faithfulness are also our hope, for we are a baptized people. For us the promises of God are real and alive. We are a baptized people and we needn't be greedy or callous or silent and the violent ways of our world need not be our norms for living. God's grace gives us the means to live according to his standards of conduct instead of ours.

Jesus was killed for telling stories, my professor once said in class. What he didn't say that day was that Jesus' own story, his death, is what gives us life. New life. I guess we all have an off-day sometimes. Thank God that God doesn't. Amen.

Some Last Things

Epilogue

On the Sunday Baptism of our Lord or the mission fair Sunday, it may be appropriate to have an affirmation of baptism liturgy. Many denominations offer such liturgies in the occasional services section of their worship books.

The Second or Third Sunday of Easter may be used to celebrate the new life that is born into the congregation through the Lenten commitments of its people. Small displays with some items requested during the mission fair may be set up in the sanctuary. Special prayers and music can serve to make the connection between the new life given to God's people at Easter and the new life members of the congregation have received and given to others through their service.

Instead of using the *Come And See* resource during Epiphany and Lent, parish leaders may wish to consider its use during the fall. The mission fair is also appropriate for a fall start-up Sunday. The relative brevity of the playlets make them suitable for use during the church school hour. They can serve as the basis for discussions about the mission and vision of the congregation. The Bible studies can be used for the same purpose as well as in preparation for a fall stewardship emphasis.

We have found it important to include children and youth in the programs of the resource. Young people can serve as players for the playlets. Some mission fair commitments can be especially geared toward children. These disciplines may include making cards for or writing letters to the shut-ins of the congregation; serving as ushers or greeters on Sunday mornings; collecting aluminum cans in the neighborhood.